JÜRGEN KLOPP

NOTES ON A SEASON

JÜRGEN KLOPP

NOTES ON A SEASON

Reach Sport
www.reachsport.com

First published in Great Britain in 2022 by
Reach Sport, 5 St Paul's Square, Liverpool, L3 9SJ.

www.reachsport.com
@reach_sport

Reach Sport is a part of Reach plc.
One Canada Square, Canary Wharf, London, E15 5AP.

ISBN: 978-1-914197-54-3

Compiled by: Roy Gilfoyle
Proofread by: Chris McLoughlin
Artwork by: Rick Cooke

Printed and bound by CPI Group (UK) Ltd,
Croydon, CR0 4YY.

NOTES ON A SEASON

2021-22

EXTRAORDINARY JOURNEY ENDS WITH TWO TROPHIES, EMPTY WALLETS AND EVEN GREATER MUTUAL LOVE

THREE finals. Two trophies. Three trips to Wembley. Sixty-three games with only four defeats. Comprehensive home and away wins against their biggest local rivals. Amazing football. Brilliant players to enjoy. Lasting memories. A bond between manager, fans and the club strengthened even further.

Don't let anyone tell you the 2021-22 season wasn't a success for Liverpool FC.

The campaign was as special as it was long. It may not have ended in the way fans, players or Jürgen Klopp would have hoped, but that shouldn't detract from a season that saw the Reds strengthen their position as the most trophy-laden English team of all time.

And by the time the disappointment of the Champions League final defeat to Real Madrid at the end of May had begun to subside, hundreds of thousands of people were ready to line the streets of Liverpool to show their heroes what their efforts had meant to them.

Klopp had spoken earlier in the season about loving the fact that Liverpool fans are not glory hunters; they are, in fact, 'journey hunters'.

He said: "Being journey hunters brings its own energy. It means you get to enjoy the moment and be in every moment. I can't think of a time when it's more important to channel this."

And what a journey it turned out to be.

The fact that the word 'quadruple' was being seriously spoken about in relation to the possibilities opening up to the Reds from early in 2022 until the middle of May tells you that this was an incredible season.

The Champions League group draw wasn't kind but the Reds emerged from a quartet that included AC Milan, Porto and Atletico Madrid as the first English team ever to gain maximum points from their six games.

Another remarkable Premier League season saw the Reds lose only two matches and finish with 92 points – enough to win the title in 23 of the previous 29 seasons.

Highlights were plenty. A four-goal first-half blitz saw

home fans streaming out of Old Trafford by half-time in an eventual 5-0 win against Manchester United. Mo Salah recorded a hat-trick that day and scored barely-believable individual goals in successive games against Manchester City and Watford during another season where he'd claim the Golden Boot with 23 league strikes.

Liverpool put another four past United in April, and five days later they completed a league double over Everton.

This was a season, don't forget, when the club lost key players to the Africa Cup of Nations for around a month, and had COVID issues to contend with that left them without star performers for some big games.

There were big boosts along the way too. Luis Diaz arrived from Porto at the end of January to add flair to an already-exciting forward line while the whole club got a massive lift in April when Klopp and crucial members of his staff signed contract extensions.

By this time the fans were making little secret of their ever-flourishing love for their manager, as 'I'm in love with him and I feel fine' was sung with greater regularity and volume with each passing game.

And the German's fist pumps to the Kop were becoming more common too as each result – at Anfield and elsewhere – became more and more important.

From January 2nd until the final game against Wolves,

the Reds would play 19 league matches, drawing only three and winning the rest to push Manchester City's title defence to its very limit – all while maintaining three cup runs that would lead them to a hat-trick of finals.

The first silverware was won in February after an epic penalty shoot-out against Chelsea that saw Caoimhin Kelleher emerge as the hero.

The sides would meet again under the Wembley arch in May for a similar outcome. Dua Lipa's 'One Kiss' was becoming a gloriously familiar victory anthem.

One of many banners that caught the eye as fans travelled the country and the continent following their team contained a picture of Klopp with the words 'Making Us All Skint Since 2015'. Trips to Italy, Portugal and Spain in the knock-out rounds of the Champions League damaged bank balances further before a Paris final that would end in disappointment.

But Klopp and his journey hunters had one final trip – back to Liverpool for a trophy parade that everyone deserved to enjoy.

This book is a reminder of every step of that journey, through Jürgen's matchday programme notes and his thoughts on each of the 63 matches.

"I love you all," said Klopp on seeing the mass of red bodies that had come to salute the club's efforts that day.

There is no doubt that the feeling is mutual.

AUG

2021

A solid start to the season saw the Reds pick up seven points from the nine available in August – but the chance to play in front of a packed Anfield and its expectant fans again pleased the boss as much as anything else

14th: Norwich City (PL) A
21st: Burnley (PL) H
28th: Chelsea (PL) H

Saturday, August 14th, 5.30pm
Premier League
Norwich City 0, Liverpool 3

Goals: Jota (26), Firmino (65), Salah (74)

Line-up: Alisson, Alexander-Arnold, Matip, Van Dijk, Tsimikas, Oxlade-Chamberlain (Fabinho 61), Milner, Keita (Elliott 83), Salah, Jota (Firmino 61), Mane.
Subs not used: Konate, Gomez, Minamino, Origi, Woodburn, Kelleher.

Jürgen's post-match reaction: 'What you go for in the start of the season is the result. The result depends on the performance. That means we were absolutely good enough to win the game, and that was the most important thing. It was a very professional performance. I don't need a 20, 25-minute sensational spell and then losing the game – it makes no sense. You have to be in the game, you have to start the season as we did today. Having an away game against a freshly-promoted team in the fully-packed stadium for the first time, so they celebrate pretty much everything today together or wanted to celebrate, that's the situation. I'm really happy that we played how we played.'

Post-match notes

Mohamed Salah became the first player in Premier League history to score a goal on the opening week of the season five times in succession.

August 2021

v Burnley
Saturday, August 21st, 12.30pm

'I CAN MAKE A FULL COMMITMENT THAT WE WILL GO FOR EVERYTHING'

Premier League

GOOD afternoon and welcome back to Anfield for our Premier League game against Burnley.

You have no idea how good it feels to say that. Welcome back! And a full welcome. A full Anfield. With a full away support. Football is back and it's wonderful.

As part of this, we of course welcome Sean Dyche, his players, staff, officials and the fans of today's visitors to our home.

Sean and his team continue to do their thing. They arguably punch above their weight season after season. They maximise their resources. They are smart. They are streetwise. They are an established Premier League force and a side that no one relishes facing.

And trust me, as a coach, that last part is something we all aspire to. I want Liverpool to be a side that opposition teams dread playing against.

Burnley will arrive today with confidence and belief. They won here last season and that will be in their thoughts, I'm sure. Yes, it was an empty Anfield but that's not to mitigate the result. Burnley will have added energy today also with the fans being back in. So having crowds back doesn't make either side weaker – it makes us all stronger. We must be ready. We must assume our opponent is stronger and hungrier than they were last season. We must assume they are a greater threat. We must know we have to work harder than ever before against them if we want the right result.

Last week against Norwich City was a big learning experience for us. We didn't start the game well and I'm sure a part of that was us all adapting to the 'new' environment we face with the return of capacity attendance.

It was helpful for us to have the two home friendlies before the campaign got underway and it did serve as a measure of re-acclimatising. But nothing compares to when it's for real. And that will be today.

For a start, the dynamic today is different because Burnley have their people here also. That changes things. We saw that at Carrow Road – the away support gave energy and verve to the boys. Away support makes atmospheres more complete.

I want to thank those who made the incredibly long trip to Norfolk to support us. The noise that came out of the away section had a noticeable impact on the boys. They even discussed it in the dressing room afterwards, how much it influenced them on the pitch.

We do not take that for granted, ever – but even more so after a season of empty stadiums and being apart. That being said, I cannot ignore one aspect that was not welcome and must be addressed.

I have to admit, I was unaware during the game and even immediately after about the song aimed at Billy Gilmour on the basis of him being a Chelsea player. I saw the club and its LGBT+ group Kop Outs! spoke about it afterwards, so I wanted to understand better. Let me add my voice to those saying please stop it and stop it immediately. I'm sure those who joined in thinking it was only 'having a go at' Chelsea will be surprised at the idea that they were part of something which was homophobic, but I would say listen to the organisations that have a proper understanding and learn.

I am 54 and without question in my life I will have said many things which offended without that being my intention. But I also hope if someone explained to me why saying it hurt them, I would do my best to stop it.

Even if the last thing I ever intended when saying it was to be hateful or hurtful…the fact it causes others to feel that way means we must listen, learn and change behaviour.

You can put me on the list of people who can improve in this way, as a person. So I feel able to say to our supporters come on, this song has no place at Liverpool or in football. Let's all try and be better together.

On the pitch, there was lots to like about how we approached our work. I thought the performance showed humility and that is encouraging. If you've followed our pre-season you will no doubt have heard or read how pleased I was with the effort and commitment of the players. They have shown desire and focus, thrown themselves into every session.

We know to be successful we have to treat each game like it is the only one that matters. Yes, it's a cliché but it's true – each match must be a cup final for us. And the best way to make sure you have this mentality when the game comes is to have it each day in training.

Being away from home for 28 days wasn't comfortable for players or staff but the attitude was without fault. Honestly, my respect for this group was already high, but now it goes to a new level.

There is so much focus on transfers and recruitment in football and particularly in the Premier League. It might not always seem so when I speak to the media, but I do understand it.

I'm a football fan as well and I'm guilty of being attracted to a story about which team might sign which player. The difference is I don't have that 'itch' when it comes to us.

I don't for one second criticise anyone – be it fan, pundit, journalist or players and coaches – for getting drawn into the allure of transfers. But as the manager of this team and a leader of this club I must always view these things with proper perspective.

We have exceptional players. We have long-term commitments from the majority of them. We have recruited smartly both this season and last. We have an elite environment and a home ground, with an atmosphere which is the envy of most.

We have so much to be optimistic about. To be joyful about. Does that guarantee success? Of course not! This is football and specifically it is the Premier League – the most competitive in the world.

Other teams are strong but they always have been. Winning in England is hard but it always has been. It's why our club's history is so special.

I make no promises on what we will achieve, where we will finish or what we might win. But I can make a full commitment that we will go with all we have and we go for everything.

We have the players, staff and club atmosphere to go for it all. We have the power and belief to make this season very special.

But what makes this place special is the appreciation of the journey. A friend of mine who is closer to the fan culture than I could ever profess to be, said to me that people support Liverpool not because they are glory hunters but because they are journey hunters.

I love this sentiment.

Our 2021/22 journey is underway and we should enjoy every second of it. Not because we know we will have success or we expect it – but because we chase it together, as a collective.

It feels like an adventure again and that is a wonderful sensation after so long apart.

Welcome back – we've missed you like crazy.

Liverpool 2, Burnley 0

Goals: Jota (18), Mane (69)

Line-up: Alisson, Alexander-Arnold, Matip, Van Dijk, Tsimikas (Gomez 90+2), Elliott, Henderson, Keita (Thiago 81), Salah, Jota (Firmino 81) Mane. Subs not used: Konate, Adrian, Jones, Minamino, Robertson, Kelleher

Jürgen's post-match reaction: 'Everybody was really looking forward to this football festival, to this game, and I think nobody leaves this place today with any kind of disappointment because I think all of our dreams were fulfilled today, atmosphere-wise. That was, for sure, the best 12.30pm atmosphere we had. It was pretty special, really special. How the game was as well, pretty special, because Burnley are Burnley – and Burnley cause you problems. And Burnley caused us problems. We played a good game, we scored two, could have scored more. Yes, we needed Ali in moments as well, even when the best save he had was offside before, but it was anyway a sensational save. Harvey was part of this performance. Everybody wants to talk to me about Harvey and I understand absolutely – when an 18-year-old boy plays such a mature game I can understand why everyone was asking, but I was not surprised he played like this. That is exactly how he has trained now for six or seven weeks since we are back, since he is back from loan. Yes, it was good.'

Post-match notes

This was the first time in 528 days that the Reds were able to play in front of a capacity Anfield crowd.

v Chelsea
Saturday, August 28th, 5.30pm

'THE EXPLOSIVE ROAR WHEN THE FIRST WHISTLE WENT WILL LIVE WITH ME FOREVER'

Premier League

GOOD afternoon and welcome back to Anfield for our Premier League fixture against Chelsea.

I would also like to specifically welcome Thomas Tuchel, his players, staff, officials and supporters of the visitors to our home.

First of all, I must say a huge congratulations to Thomas, his team and the club on becoming European champions last season and winning the UEFA Super Cup this. We know better than most how difficult that achievement is and what it means when it happens.

I've written in this column previously and said exhaustively in the media how much I admire Thomas and his work. Undoubtedly he is one of the best coaches in world football. He didn't need to win the Champions League for most of us in the game to realise this, but it certainly makes the point even more pronounced.

It's clear from his demeanour in public how settled he already is in English football. He has taken to Chelsea and the Premier League and obviously it has been reciprocated.

Chelsea are a super-powerful opponent and one we must respect. World-class players back to front. World-class leadership in the dugout. A club used to winning in the modern era. A very powerful combination. But respect is an important word and sentiment and I'm sure no one at Chelsea sees playing Liverpool as a footballing holiday.

This fixture coming so early in the season is a challenge for both of us, but neither gets to pick the schedule so here we are. And what a contest. Honestly, it is something for us to relish and look forward to. That's my attitude and I'm sure it will be similar for our opponents.

The game doesn't need to be made bigger than it is. It is big. That's cool. But all any team can win today is three points. That is the maximum.

I know the narrative built around it will be bigger and that's fine. 'Making a statement' and so on. It all adds to the drama. But we, as a team, cannot be distracted by any of that.

It's very important we focus entirely on our jobs, influencing what we can and do it the best we can. I am always at peace with the outcome when that happens.

We have played two matches so far and there have been important learnings from both. I don't for one second think we are even close to perfect at this stage, but frankly it would be odd if we were.

There were things I liked in both games, things I didn't, things I think we did well and things I think we can do better. That is pretty normal and I'm sure Chelsea will have felt the same with their fixtures.

What I really liked in both games is that the players immediately recognised the importance the entire squad has to play this campaign if we are to stand any chance at all of being successful. The levels in training from those who haven't appeared as frequently on the team-sheet yet have been just as high as those who have. This is critically important.

At the time of writing this I genuinely don't know what combination we will go with, but I have total confidence that whoever is selected will be ready. Also, I know that all 20 names who are involved today, in whatever capacity, will have a role to play.

Every contribution is as important as the next. We must have this collective approach, not just for each game but every day we are together.

Of course the supporters are also key to this collective effort and I don't think there is any need for a rousing team-talk for Anfield today. We have spoken a lot about the importance of focusing the energy in a positive way on us and leaving behind any ignorant, prejudicial chants. But Anfield has probably never been more important to us than it is right now.

Honestly, for the Burnley game the explosive roar when the first whistle went will live with me for the rest of my life. It was a noise full of emotion, belief and anticipation. I am getting goosebumps thinking about it again now. And not just that. The way the fans celebrated us winning the ball back and players sprinting to close spaces. The way each and every player was treated like it was team's star person.

This is where our support can be the difference. It's a support that is smart and savvy and recognises how and when it can play its part.

When you face an opponent like the one we do today there will be periods, for sure, where we are under pressure. To have a crowd who have your back in those moments, rather than be on your back, is so valuable.

I say all this in the knowledge that the responsibility starts and ends with us, though. The team. Players and management. It's for us to inspire you and it's for us to make sure your energy is focused on a group of people whose minimum requirement is to give all they have from the first whistle until the last.

I am super-excited for this opportunity today and I hope we can do ourselves and our supporters justice with the performance we produce. And that's really all you can ever hope for and certainly all you can ever promise.

Enjoy every second of it.

Liverpool 1, Chelsea 1

Goal: Salah (45+5pen)

Line-up: Alisson, Alexander-Arnold, Matip, Van Dijk, Robertson (Tsimikas 86), Elliott, Fabinho, Henderson (Thiago 74), Salah, Firmino (Jota 43), Mane.
Subs not used: Konate, Keita, Gomez, Oxlade-Chamberlain, Minamino, Kelleher

Jürgen's post-match reaction: 'I liked the game. Look, a few years ago, we won I think 2-1 or 2-0 against Chelsea and Mo Salah fired the ball in the far corner, which is actually not a chance – a nice goal, but not a chance. Today we had obviously bigger chances in the first half already which we didn't score from, that means the performance was really good against the strongest Chelsea side for a long, long time. It was always difficult against Chelsea and it's now difficult against Chelsea, so I was really happy with the first half. And the second half… I'm not somebody who watches football from time to time and thinks, 'Oh, 11 versus 10, that must be easy.' I saw five million games and know that is really not a massive advantage, especially against a quality side like Chelsea with the defending skills they have and with now the job they had to do just to defend in and around the box more or less. It was tricky. We could have done better for sure, but it's early in the season, you need this one moment where you can get through, where you can finish it off.'

Post-match notes

Chelsea's Reece James was red-carded just before half-time as both sides maintained their unbeaten starts to the season.

SEP

2021

Mo Salah and Sadio Mane hit goal landmarks as the Reds built on a solid start to the season with only a draw at Brentford blotting the copybook. Two wins out of two in the Champions League and progress in the Carabao Cup were balanced against a serious injury to a youngster who had started the season in great form

12th: Leeds United (PL) A
15th: AC Milan (CL) H
18th: Crystal Palace (PL) H
21st Norwich City (CC) A
25th Brentford (PL) A
28th: Porto (CL) A

Sunday, September 12th, 4.30pm
Premier League
Leeds United 0, Liverpool 3

Goals: Salah (30), Fabinho (50), Mane (90+2)

Line-up: Alisson, Alexander-Arnold, Matip, Van Dijk, Robertson, Elliott (Henderson 63), Fabinho, Thiago (Keita 90+3), Salah, Jota (Oxlade-Chamberlain 82), Mane. Subs not used: Konate, Milner, Jones, Tsimikas, Kelleher

Jürgen's post-match reaction: 'This is not a game you can play nice like chess – you have to throw everything on the pitch to make little advantages. We did that. That's what I liked most about the game, that we were really ready – for the atmosphere today, the intensity Leeds are asking for. It's a really tough place to come and we did really well. We played here last year and now a third time, this was the most convincing performance so far. Last year we won at home, yes, it was more spectacular. And an away game here without a crowd is obviously a completely different cup of tea. So, yes, I'm happy with the performance.'

Post-match notes

Mohamed Salah scored his 100th goal in the Premier League. Harvey Elliott was badly injured after a challenge by Pascal Struijk that saw the Leeds player sent off.

Jürgen Klopp

v AC Milan
Wednesday, September 15th, 8pm

'YOU RECOGNISE TRUE LEADERSHIP IN A CRISIS. SIMON [KJAER] SHONE THAT TRAUMATIC DAY'

UEFA Champions League

September 2021

GOOD evening and welcome back to Anfield for our opening UEFA Champions League game against AC Milan. I welcome Stefano Pioli, his players, staff and the officials of our visitors from Italy to our home.

As fixtures go, this is one where the very mention of the two team names makes you realise you are in line for a proper occasion. Such amazing heritage for both. And a famous joint history in this very competition.

I must say the Champions League is a better competition for having AC Milan back in. Honestly speaking, I would sooner they be in someone else's group because they are so strong, but now we face each other we must embrace the challenge.

Stefano has done a fantastic job at Milan and is a tremendously experienced coach and leader.

At the time of writing these notes, Serie A, like the Premier League, is only a few games in, but AC Milan have already made an impressive start. They look strong, organised and full of belief. They are such a powerful opponent. World-class players in their ranks. Street-wise. The full package.

I am doing this column before we play Leeds United, and so therefore cannot comment on either the result or performance.

There is an issue around this that I want to address, though, on which we received clarification late on Friday evening last week. We have seen with the recent international-break confusion and worry around call-ups. This will come again in October and November and possibly even January and March.

Let me make it clear that I love that my players have earned the honour and prestige of being able to play for their country. I was never good enough as a player to have this privilege, but I know it's recognition players strive for and work hard to achieve.

Yes, in press conferences around international weeks I often comment, when asked, that waiting for them to come back is like a parent waiting for their children to return home safely. But I have never and will never be a block on this ambition and neither will the club. In an ideal world every single one of my players is called up for their country. This is our hope and dream for each of them.

But at the moment it's not about injuries and game-load. It is, though, about calendars, commitments and demands on these boys. These conversations are important and we must continue to look for solutions. We all have a duty on this. There is at the moment a spotlight due to global issues and restrictions around travelling and entry into countries and territories.

The last few weeks – and it will be the same in October and maybe November – was about something beyond all of our control really. It was about the ongoing issues of trying to play football across the planet while the pandemic is still here and travelling is far from straightforward.

It was also about the pressures of fulfilling a schedule that has been pushed to breaking point over the past 18 months.

For the last break we had four players affected to different degrees. Mo Salah for Egypt, plus Bobby Firmino, Fabinho and Alisson Becker for Brazil. All of these boys would do anything within their power to represent their nations. They are passionate for their country.

Honestly, in English I struggle to find the words to express how frustrated I felt for them that they found themselves placed in this position.

I only pray that the fans in Brazil – and for Mo, the Egyptian supporters – recognise the players are faultless in this. In fact it's more than that – they are the ones who suffer the most despite doing nothing wrong. They are punished for factors beyond their control. And yes, beyond Liverpool FC's control also.

There are restrictions on where you can travel and how you can return which means it cannot be business as usual. For our players affected it cannot be ignored that they live and work in the UK. With no exemption in place, what else could they and we do?

I empathise totally with the Brazilian and Egyptian team management. I would want these four amazing players to report also. The fans in their country deserve to have their best players compete so they can qualify for a World Cup. But at the moment COVID is still with us.

I understand by the time this column is public I will have probably spoken a lot about this and the politics around it. And also decisions around the calendar that do need to be looked at. But I wanted to use these pages to make it clear that inflicting further pain on the players is wrong and should not be in anyone's mind if we have this situation later in the month also.

The players deserve that the people in power find solutions and not make them collateral damage.

Before we know it we will be discussing the October call-ups and this whole situation will be back. And it's more than just about quarantine exemption, although of course that is a critical problem to sort out.

Trying to cram in these extra matches will also impact. Common sense and solution-based thinking must be at the forefront of the discussions. It cannot be right that matches can kick off so late in the second international week and then clubs be expected to play on Saturday – or in our case after the next break early Saturday.

The practical impact of this means we will be without these players. It's not right and it needs to be addressed.

Finally, I am usually more keen to focus on my own players rather than an opponent, but tonight I must make an exception. This evening it is possible that Simon Kjaer will line up against us and this is a person who I think has the respect of the entire football and sporting world.

You recognise true leadership in a crisis. I think the world acknowledges this now more than ever with everything that goes on around us.

Like millions of others I was rocked by the scenes that unfolded at the European Championship in the summer when Christian Eriksen fell ill during Denmark's opening group game.

There were many heroes that night, not least of all the remarkable medical professionals for the Danish national team, in the stadium and subsequently at the hospital. But Simon shone that traumatic day for his own conduct.

The image of the Danish players shielding their team-mate as he was cared for will, in my opinion, forever be one of the most iconic in sporting history. It showed the best of humanity. Compassion, care and love for their friend.

Honestly, I have no idea how he managed to not only keep his own composure in that situation, but to have the clarity of mind to make the decisions he did in that moment. His conduct humbles us all.

I'm told that Simon's dad is an LFC fan – and if that is the case he must be bursting with pride that his boy is now recognised worldwide as the epitome of our anthem 'You'll Never Walk Alone'.

I know our supporters are knowledgeable and generous of spirit and therefore I am sure Simon will feel the gratitude of the home crowd tonight, but for the 90-plus minutes of the game he is again the opponent.

It will be so cool just before kick-off to hear that Champions League anthem and see the players lined up in front of a full Anfield. We missed supporters for every second of every game during the pandemic, but I must admit it was most acute on the European nights.

Let's have all the noise, all the colour, all the positive energy and all the passion and intensity that is our trademark. Let's give this fixture the stage it deserves.

I honestly cannot wait.

Liverpool 3, AC Milan 2

Goals: Tomori (9og), Salah (48), Henderson (69)

Line-up: Alisson, Alexander-Arnold, Matip, Gomez, Robertson, Henderson (Milner 84), Fabinho, Keita, (Thiago 71), Salah (Oxlade-Chamberlain 84), Origi (Mane 63), Jota (Jones 71). Subs not used: Van Dijk, Konate, Adrian, Minamino, Tsimikas, Phillips, Kelleher

Jürgen's post-match reaction: 'It was a brilliant game, very exciting and very entertaining. With 10 or 15 minutes where we lost a little bit the plot, whatever. We were not compact enough anymore, we got carried away with our own football, pretty much, and made it then complicated – which we shouldn't have done – in our possession. Last line slightly too deep; midfield didn't close the gaps anymore and stuff like this. So they could pass through, they scored two goals. In a moment like this, obviously the game can be decided but not tonight because we could adjust in half-time and did that. Played again really good football and scored two wonderful goals, so won the game. Everyone knew before already but now probably definitely everybody knows: AC Milan came from Pot 4 in this group – very funny! So, that's the quality in the group. It's really good that we won this game tonight because obviously you need each point in this group to get through.'

Post-match notes

Mohamed Salah scored one but missed a penalty – only his second failure from 19 spot-kicks for Liverpool.

Jürgen Klopp

v Crystal Palace
Saturday, September 18th, 3pm

'LOOK AT WHAT WE HAVE AND TELL ME OUR SQUAD CAN'T COMPETE FOR EVERYTHING'

Premier League

September 2021

GOOD afternoon and welcome back to Anfield for our Premier League game against Crystal Palace. I welcome Patrick Vieira, his players and staff as well as the officials and supporters of our visitors.

Patrick will know this ground well as a player. He will have enjoyed many battles here during his incredible playing career.

Today is his first time coming to face Liverpool in a competitive game as a manager but I'm certain he will arrive with the same determination, expectation and ambition that has defined him as one of the game's all-time great competitors.

Although he is new to the Premier League in management terms, he has solid experience behind him spanning five years leading a senior team now, across three very different countries and leagues.

I've been a big admirer from afar for what he has done at New York and Nice.

Of course it is early for him at Palace and they have undergone a lot of changes over the summer, but it is already apparent he and his staff are putting their own stamp on the club.

It is clear he has philosophy and a direction of how he wants his teams to approach a contest. They were outstanding against Tottenham, even when it was 11 versus 11, so we are in for a really hard game today.

Someone who unfortunately can't feature for us this

afternoon is Harvey Elliott. I'm conscious a lot has been said and written on this already and I actually think Harv will benefit from a break in the endless publicity around what happened, but I do want to address it in this column.

I don't need to go over the incident itself. It's in the past now. Harvey has had the surgery, it's been a success and each day that passes is a day closer to him being able to play football for Liverpool again.

He is an extraordinary young person and has a wonderful loving family around him. He'll want for nothing in the support and care stakes. For him, he must now treat his rehab as he has approached everything else in his career so far. Attack it with positivity and with a desire to listen, learn and improve.

He has the world's best support staff around him during this and he will be back in great shape. Until then, we wait for him.

We are in a very intense period for the squad now. It's not the most intense period but it is the start of the constant intensity as regards the schedule. It's game after game now for most of these boys for a very long time. It's not to complain. We are all used to it.

There is also an element of this which is a positive. The more busy our calendar and the players' own commitments, it means we are all being successful. We want to be in as many competitions as we can qualify for, for as long as possible. I have never hidden from my personal view that individuals can't win anything in this sport. Even a starting eleven can't. To be successful you have to have a squad where every member contributes.

'Squad depth' has been a vogue topic for people to debate since the summer. As I have said in media conferences, I am not interested and have no time for pointless comparisons with rival teams. This is the Premier League – every squad is powerful.

It is possible to respect the strength of an opponent without it impacting on your own. I have total faith in ours. Absolute belief. Look at what we have and tell me our squad can't compete for everything.

What's cool is that we get the opportunity to show those who doubt it that they are premature in their judgement. I like this. It's a challenge.

In terms of picking line-ups during this period, I admit there is a balance between stability of selection, which can give a team rhythm, and the freshness that results from making suitable changes at the appropriate time.

This is very much my responsibility, plus my coaches'. We relish it. But of course, as with everything we do, we share the challenge with our players. We make the decisions but they have to be ready to grasp opportunity when it comes.

Honestly, the level they show in each and every

training session at the moment tells me they understand what they need to do, as a collective, perfectly. They push each other, they inspire each other, they support each other and they have the perfect balance of desire and control in everything they do.

A player who epitomises our insatiable appetite to achieve more, recorded an incredible milestone at Elland Road last week. Mo Salah scored his 100th Premier League goal that afternoon. Because of what happened with Harvey we weren't really in the celebration mood immediately after. But we needed to recognise this remarkable feat as a collective.

The next day at the training ground we all came together to congratulate him.

What a player, what a professional, what a person.

We appreciate him so much you cannot believe. I remember on the final day of last season, when he just missed out on the Golden Boot, our dressing room was so gutted for him, because of all he'd done for us during a really tough season to keep us in the race.

He really is an inspirational figure and as a club we have benefited so much from his hunger for goals. And that's not to forget all his assists.

I don't understand cricket at all. I really don't. But I believe '100 not out' is a phrase that is connected to that sport? That's Mo…100 on the board but more to come.

Finally, the atmosphere inside Anfield on Wednesday

for the Champions League night can only be described as vintage stuff. It was superb.

Today we are back to league action and a 3pm kick-off. Let's try and bring the Champions League vibe.

Noise and passion from the moment you come in to the moment you leave.

We plan to play in a manner that means we join you in lighting our home up in the best way possible.

Liverpool 3, Crystal Palace 0

Goals: Mane (43), Salah (78), Keita (89)

Line-up: Alisson, Milner, Konate, Van Dijk, Tsimikas, Henderson (Origi 88), Fabinho, Thiago (Keita 62), Salah, Jota (Jones 76), Mane. Subs not used: Gomez, Oxlade-Chamberlain, Minamino, Robertson, Phillips, Kelleher.

Jürgen's post-match reaction: 'That Mo scored should not be a massive surprise. Sadio scored for the ninth time in a row against Crystal Palace, which is exceptional, and he scored his 100th goal for Liverpool in all competitions, which is exceptional. Naby Keita scored the most wonderful goal of all three, so that's all important for us. But I told the boys after the game that this was one of the most hard-fought 3-0s I ever saw. We had to give absolutely everything. So, I'm really pleased, I'm really pleased. In a season, when you are Liverpool, you win football games from time to time. When you win, usually you are really good or brilliant. Today we were not brilliant but we were good. We accepted the battle Crystal Palace was here for and that's why I am really happy about the result, really happy about the performance. This Sunday-Wednesday-Saturday rhythm is just the most tricky one in the Premier League and so that we came through that now in the moment is very important, with all the changes we had to make and one we didn't want to make but that worked out really well with Millie at right-back. So, it was not brilliant, but really good and I liked that.'

Post-match notes

Sadio Mane scored his 100th Liverpool goal. It was also his ninth successive goalscoring game against Crystal Palace.

Tuesday, September 21st, 7.45pm
Carabao Cup third round
Norwich City 0, Liverpool 3

Goals: Minamino (4, 80), Origi (50)

Line-up: Kelleher, Bradley, Konate, Gomez, Tsimikas (Robertson 66), Oxlade-Chamberlain, Jones (Henderson 87), Keita (Morton 46), Gordon, Origi, Minamino. Subs not used: Adrian, Jota, Phillips, Balagizi

Jürgen's post-match reaction: 'We started really well and I liked that - really aggressive, really lively, but then you could see we didn't train because we had to make a lot of decisions really late. The last line and the goalie saved us in these moments with speed, good challenges and stuff like that, so there was not really something in it for Norwich. We scored a goal, a really good goal again after a set-piece, a massive ball, massive. Half-time we had to change and Naby had kicked the grass, a little... sort of thing, we are not too concerned but we had to change. Then, we had Curtis in the half-space and Tyler in the six and it looked much [more] natural immediately so then the boys passed quicker, passed smarter and we changed Oxlade, a little bit higher on the pitch on the left wing, and Taki, who is obviously in really good shape, more in the centre and half-spaces so Ox could use his speed and Taki connected the game together with Tyler and Curtis. So, it was all good, we scored the second and third goals and controlled the game, which was absolutely brilliant.'

Saturday, September 25th, 5.30pm
Premier League
Brentford 3, Liverpool 3

Goals: Jota (31), Salah (54), Jones (67)

Line-up: Alisson, Alexander-Arnold, Matip, Van Dijk, Robertson, Henderson, Fabinho, Jones (Firmino 68), Salah, Jota, Mane. Subs not used: Konate, Milner, Gomez, Oxlade-Chamberlain, Minamino, Tsimikas, Origi, Kelleher

Jürgen's post-match reaction: 'A wild, wild game. Offensively, I am really happy. I think in moments we played some of the best football we've played so far this season; we created top chances against a really well organised side. They were very good, but obviously we struggled tonight with their long balls. I was not too happy with how we started the game and that's how we conceded the goal, a little bit. It was a situation where we could have been more organised. It's not so easy, but [we needed] to be much more composed in this situation to win these little challenges. They scored at the second post; there was no space to score, but they did. We reacted well, scored really nice goals. The second half, we controlled the game better, but in the phase where we maybe played the best football, they scored the equaliser. The 2-1 for Mo was outstanding; a super pass from Fab, who had so many good football moments. The goal from Curtis, outstanding, but because we didn't finish the game off the door stayed open and they used it again. They stayed in the game and it was really tricky for us tonight because usually when you play that well, you can control the game better but we couldn't because the goalie chipped one ball in behind always in our last line and they did really well with these balls – with the first and second balls – so you never can really control it and that made it tricky. They deserved their three goals and they deserved the point. I think we could have scored more; they could have scored one more, we could have scored four or five more and it would have been even more spectacular. But it's fine, we got a point, they got a point, let's carry on.'

Post-match notes

Mohamed Salah scored his 100th Premier League goal for Liverpool.

Tuesday, September 28th, 8pm
UEFA Champions League
Porto 1, Liverpool 5

Goals: Salah (18, 60), Mane (45), Firmino (77, 81)

Line-up: Alisson, Milner (Gomez 66), Matip, Van Dijk, Robertson, Henderson (Oxlade-Chamberlain 73), Fabinho, Jones, Salah (Firmino 67), Jota (Origi 88), Mane (Minamino 67). Subs not used: Konate, Keita, Adrian, Tsimikas, Phillips, Kelleher, N Williams

Jürgen's post-match reaction: 'We had a tricky start because obviously Porto watched the Brentford game, started pretty direct. We struggled a little bit in the beginning but that's the reason why we didn't make a lot of changes, that's because I wanted that we find the feedback on the pitch and sort the situation there and that's what we did. From a specific moment on we played really good football. We didn't use our big chances, we used two half-chances to score, to be 2-0 up. But we had really good football moments. We played, really, some good football and scored nice goals, but had even better chances. So, it's all good for tonight.'

Post-match notes

Five more goals meant the Reds had scored 20 goals in their six matches in September.

OCT

2021

Another unbeaten month saw the Reds continue their progress in the cup competitions but October was most memorable for matches against the Manchester clubs – and one in particular that emptied Old Trafford much earlier than usual

3rd: Manchester City (PL) H
16th: Watford (PL) A
19th: Atletico Madrid (CL) A
24th: Manchester United (PL) A
27th: Preston North End (CC) A
30th: Brighton (PL) H

v Manchester City
Sunday, October 3rd, 4.30pm

'TODAY IS A REAL CHALLENGE. IT'S A PROPER GAME. BRILLIANT. I LOVE THIS'

Premier League

October 2021

GOOD afternoon and welcome to Anfield for our match against Manchester City. I also welcome Pep Guardiola, his players and staff as well as the officials and supporters of our visitors.

Like most seasons, any mention of Pep in my programme column must also come with congratulations. They arrive as reigning champions of our league after producing some amazing football last season in very difficult circumstances. How they performed and the consistency they showed is a testament to the quality of their team obviously, but also their character and desire. And, of course, the leadership of Pep and his coaches.

Our respect for them, as a team and club, could not be higher. The toughest opponent imaginable.

And for Pep personally, I saw he now has the most wins of any manager in the history of Manchester City.

It is clear when you meet and speak to him how much he feels for this club and despite all the remarkable accolades he has already gained in football, as a player and as a coach, I'm sure this particular one will mean a lot.

So today is a real challenge. It's a proper game. Brilliant. I love this.

We are at our home, facing the current champions and we will attack it with all we have. This is why football is such an amazing sport. Occasions like this.

I mentioned respect earlier and it's an important theme on days like today. We respect them, of course, but it is at a healthy level. It is possible to have this without needing to diminish our own qualities.

Let me be clear. I think we are a proper team also. I think we can beat any team in the world on any given day. That's how good we are also. It's two heavyweights. We don't need a puncher's chance.

We are powerful, we are ambitious, we are hungry for more and we have some of the best players in the world in our dressing room.

We have leaders from front to back that will be heading into today with nothing other than positive anticipation. And why not?

We view the 'pressure' around occasions like this as a positive feeling. It's opportunity!

We should start each season craving pressure games like this. It means we are in the race. It means we fight for things that are special.

This sort of pressure brings energy if you view it as such. Other players and professionals across the planet will be watching today and wishing they were part of this. It's pressure which has been earned by these amazing, talented footballers, from both sides.

I know at the time of reading this column the contest itself will have been built up to meaning something far more than 'just' three points.

This is the outside world of which we have no control. The usual rhetoric we hear around blockbuster games. Who is going to make a 'statement' and so on?

But that mentality doesn't exist in the dressing room. All that can be won today is three Premier League points. That's it. And that's enough of a motivation for us I can tell you.

The game is worthy of hype and billing, of course it is. But not because of what it might mean come May. It's because of what it will mean on Sunday evening.

It's so cool this fixture again has a full stadium to witness it. The players deserve this. Anfield knows its importance. It will direct its energy towards us. Supporting us. The focus entirely on us and what we are doing and how they can help. We know we will need it.

Before the game, though, we will pause to pay tribute to a person who is as responsible as anyone for making occasions like today matter as much as they do to Liverpool Football Club.

Sir Roger Hunt, who died peacefully this week, was a true giant. Since I have been in Liverpool I have tried to learn as much as I can about the people who built this institution on their talent, commitment, personality and achievements. The legends whose shoulders we stand on.

Sir Roger is someone whose contribution can be

equalled by other legends but not surpassed. His goals lifted Bill Shankly's team into the top-flight and then to securing league titles and an FA Cup.

How he played meant he set the standards from the front of the pitch. His natural ability was matched by an attitude of working harder than anyone else and doing all you could to help your team and team-mates.

Everything I hear from those who remember seeing him play says he would have thrived in our team.

I hope the outpouring of love and appreciation brings comfort to his family. I hope they again see why the Liverpool fans choose to honour him as a 'Sir'.

I saw a quote from him saying that honour coming from the Kop meant more than it ever could coming from any establishment or organisation.

We stand to remember and pay tribute and then we try and play in a way he would have been proud of: be selfless, committed and adventurous.

Liverpool 2, Manchester City 2

Goals: Mane (59), Salah (76)

Line-up: Alisson, Milner (Gomez 78), Matip, Van Dijk, Robertson, Henderson, Fabinho, Jones, Salah, Jota (Firmino 68), Mane. Subs not used: Konate, Keita, Oxlade-Chamberlain, Minamino, Tsimikas, Kelleher, N Williams

Jürgen's post-match reaction: 'Quite an exciting game, with two completely different halves. Thank God that there were two halves today because the first half was exactly like you shouldn't do it against City and the second half was exactly like you should do it against City. Four goals happened in the second half but in the first half I can't remember a chance from us. Our biggest problem in the first half was we didn't play football. You meet for a football game, people come into a stadium and you don't play football – that sounds wrong and is wrong. So we needed to start playing football in the second half, we did that immediately. All of a sudden City had to run a lot, had to defend, completely different to the first half because we now played really good. If we would have played only the second half, I actually would have liked to win the game. But together with the first half I am not that cheeky, I think the point is fine. We caused them massive problems [in the second half], we were really in the game, we scored wonderful goals. The first goal is a great, great counter-attack, winning the ball, bam, bam, two passes, Sadio great position, top finish. The second goal, only the best players in the world score goals like this. The first touch, the first challenge he wins, then going there, putting it on the right foot and then finishing the situation off like he did, absolutely exceptional. Because this club never forgets anything, people will talk about this goal for a long, long time.'

Post-match notes

Anfield paid a special tribute to Roger Hunt, the Reds' second-highest scorer in history and a 1966 World Cup winner, following his passing the week before.

Saturday, October 16th, 12.30pm
Premier League
Watford 0, Liverpool 5

Goals: Mane (8), Firmino (37, 52, 90+1), Salah (54)

Line-up: Kelleher, Alexander-Arnold (Oxlade-Chamberlain 64), Matip, Van Dijk, Robertson (Tsimikas 64), Milner (N Williams 83), Henderson, Keita, Salah, Firmino, Mane. Subs not used: Konate, Gomez, Adrian, Minamino, Jota, Origi

Jürgen's post-match reaction: 'Mo is in a good shape, the three goals of Bobby were really nice, the 100th Premier League goal for Sadio and all these nice little stories, but you cannot overlook the performance of Mo today. I said it after the game, cut the goal off [and] it was [still] an outstanding performance how he played today. That's really good, very important for us and that's why we can win football games. Yes, the goal was very special, but if you go back a little bit you might find a goal against Watford at home which looks pretty similar to this one. He is obviously the kind of player who can do these kind of things. It's good for us. He's a top-class professional. He likes training – the physical part of it, the tactical side of it. He's a top, top professional. He's doing these kind of things in training as well. Our problem is that we don't have too much time for training, so usually we recover and we don't play. That means we don't see that often in training because we don't have time for it.'

Post-match notes

Bobby Firmino became the first Brazilian to net two Premier League hat-tricks after his treble at Vicarage Road. Mo Salah scored for the eighth game in a row in all competitions with his stunning solo effort. Sadio Mane netted his 100th Premier League goal. Liverpool became the first English top-flight team to score three or more times in seven consecutive away matches in all competitions. The win made it 20 games unbeaten in all competitions, stretching back to a Champions League defeat to Real Madrid in April.

Tuesday, October 19th, 8pm
UEFA Champions League
Atletico Madrid 2, Liverpool 3

Goals: Salah (8, 78pen), Keita (13)

Line-up: Alisson, Alexander-Arnold (Gomez 85), Matip, Van Dijk, Robertson, Keita (Fabinho 46), Henderson, Milner (Oxlade-Chamberlain 63), Salah (N Williams 90+2), Firmino, Mane (Jota 62). Subs not used: Konate, Adrian, Minamino, Tsimikas, Phillips, Kelleher

Jürgen's post-match reaction: 'When these two teams face each other then some drama I would say is guaranteed. Both teams are proper fighting units, are used to fighting for the things they want to reach, and that's clear. Of course, the story of the game is a special one because you don't very often, that easy, go 2-0 up against Atletico after 13 minutes. I said it now a couple of times but it's still true, the human brain can be your biggest enemy. We misunderstood that situation completely. We wanted to control the game in the wrong way, we played in the wrong spaces and obviously gave two cheap goals away. At half-time, I think everybody here in the room and who watched the game thought, 'Okay, Atletico are now on the winning side so that will go in only one direction.' But we thought, 'We are still here so let's give it a try.' I told the boys at half-time, it's really positive because we know much more now than we knew before the game about them, we just have to use the right spaces and to play in the right spaces and then everything will be fine. And the red card, of course it's unlucky but I think it's a red card – you cannot change that, the foot is in the face, that's what you get red cards for. That's not cool but it happened. That's the story of the game, pretty much. We still had to defend with all we have because even with 10 men they were quite intense to play. But the dirty three points are very often the most important, and they were dirty tonight of course. It was not our best football but we got them and that's a big step.'

Post-match notes

Mo Salah became Liverpool's record goalscorer in the Champions League, his two goals taking him to 31, one more than Steven Gerrard.

Sunday, October 24th, 4.30pm
Premier League
Manchester United 0, Liverpool 5

Goals: Keita (5), Jota (13), Salah (38, 45+5, 50)

Line-up: Alisson, Alexander-Arnold, Konate, Van Dijk, Robertson, Keita (Oxlade-Chamberlain 63), Henderson, Milner (Jones 27), Salah, Firmino (Mane 76), Jota.
Subs not used: Gomez, Adrian, Minamino, Tsimikas, Origi, Matip

Jürgen's post-match reaction: 'It's a good day, a really good day and I don't want to be disrespectful. I have no idea, but it's a big one. We know that. Obviously after the game I got told that never happened in the long history of LFC; this group always wanted to write their own little chapters for the big, big history book of this club. This one was a little one tonight, a little chapter. People will talk about it in the future, 100 per cent, because it will not happen very often, if it happens again at all. We saw the game as well and we know we were lucky in two or three situations where United could have scored in the first half. I think they should have scored the first one, but that doesn't make our performance [any less], that's just how it is. In front of the goal, in the last third, we were exceptional. We were clinical, we were ruthless, our high press was outstanding, we really won balls in great areas, the formation was top and all these kind of things you want to see as a coach, worked out really great. The difference is now that you usually don't score with each situation you have pretty much, but that's what we did and why we were 4-0 up at half-time. Second half, early 5-0 and the red card, game over, so then just control it and try to get home healthy.'

Post-match notes

Liverpool won consecutive league games by 5+ goals for the first time since 1935 when they beat Stoke 5-0 and Chelsea 6-0. Mo Salah became the first opposition player to score a Premier League hat-trick at Old Trafford as he also completed his 10th consecutive goalscoring game for the Reds.

Wednesday, October 27th, 7.45pm
Carabao Cup fourth round
Preston North End 0, Liverpool 2

Goals: Minamino (62), Origi (84)

Line-up: Adrian, N Williams, Matip (Phillips 46), Gomez, Tsimikas, Oxlade-Chamberlain (Dixon-Bonner 90+1), Morton, Jones (Beck 90+1), Blair (Bradley 55), Origi, Minamino. Subs not used: Konate, Firmino, Jota, Hughes, Pitaluga

Jürgen's post-match reaction: 'We didn't play well, that's how it is. We started quite okay, but then we lost the structure completely. We were too lively, too desperate to get the ball. Everybody dropped and we didn't have enough players between the lines. That can absolutely happen when you don't play a lot together. I saw a lot of nice individual performances; as a team we can play better, but individually I saw a few really nice performances. It's all about getting through to the next round, that's what we did. Taki [Minamino] is in an outstanding moment. He understands our game really well, so you can throw him in and he can be immediately a massive part of our football. Divock's goal was just Divock Origi.'

Post-match notes

Tyler Morton made his full debut while Harvey Blair and Owen Beck made their first senior appearances.

October 2021

v Brighton
Saturday, October 30th, 3pm

'ADAM IS ONE OF THE FOUNDING FATHERS OF THE SUCCESS THIS TEAM HAS ENJOYED'

Premier League

GOOD afternoon and welcome back to Anfield for our Premier League game against Brighton and Hove Albion. I welcome Graham Potter, his players, staff, officials and supporters of our visitors.

For those of us who have followed and admired Graham's career, albeit from a distance, it is no surprise to see the progress Brighton have made this season under his leadership.

Since he has arrived back in England to lead football teams he has always brought a clear identity to how he wants his teams to play. He is an innovator and is adventurous. His players reflect his approach. They play with courage and freedom.

We know from personal experience from last season just how dangerous they are. They came to Anfield and won and I have no problem at all in saying they deserved it.

So we need no reminder ahead of today about how we must approach the game. We respect them and we prepare to face a top side.

I cannot speak about our visitors without mentioning a crucial player within their ranks for whom we still have great affection. Adam Lallana is our opponent today and we his. We want to beat him with all we have and he will feel the same about us. So when the whistle goes our friendship and shared experiences are placed on pause. We all know this.

But I hope either side of the game there will be an opportunity for us all to show appreciation to Adam for his contribution. He came back here last season when our ground was empty. Therefore today is the first real opportunity for our supporters to acknowledge him. Again, our fans are smart enough to know while the game is on he is a pivotal player for an opposition trying to take the points.

Adam is one of the founding fathers of the success this current Liverpool side has enjoyed in recent seasons and I personally will forever be grateful for what he did when with us. It looks like now he does something similar for Brighton that he did for us. I wish him nothing but good luck for every game when he doesn't face Liverpool.

For us, it is about staying in our current mood. I am writing this column before we go to Preston in the League Cup, so I cannot comment on quality of performance or result there. However, what the players do in this moment shows me they have an intelligent grasp of what is required to continue on our current trajectory.

We have had a lot of away games since the last international break and to be honest, being back at Anfield today feels really good because it's felt like a long time since we were last together here.

The performances and results at Watford, Atletico Madrid and Manchester United were pleasing for different reasons. We showed different skills and disciplines in each of those. Each was a unique challenge and we treated it as such.

I am conscious the result last weekend in Manchester in particular will have caused excitement and that's absolutely fine. We were excited also, although for us we quickly put a lid on that.

I watched the press conference ahead of the Preston game which my assistant-manager Pep Lijnders hosted and he spoke about the reaction in the dressing room at full-time. If the past 18 months has taught us anything it is that we should enjoy special moments collectively when we can. Enjoy and cherish each other. That's what we did. But what is most telling about our group is how we reacted the next day. We closed the book on Old Trafford the very next morning and were back in work mode.

After each game – win, lose or draw – I address the squad the next morning before we train. The meeting never changes that much really. We acknowledge what has happened the previous day, good and bad, then we draw a line and move on. We immediately focus on what's next.

This has to be our mentality. From the matches we take information. We take what we can learn from – again that's positives and negatives. But we never dwell. We are never satisfied.

I love that our fans have been able to enjoy what we have done so far this season and it is their job to dream. It is ours to deliver. And to deliver what we think we are capable of, we need always to be in the moment.

I am not looking to temper or rain on optimism. I think people know me well enough to recognise that isn't who I am. But maintaining the focus on the next opponent and only the next opponent is so important for us. In times we have been successful it's been our cornerstone.

The only thing that can help you from a previous game is the information you take from it, personally and collectively. The result and even the performance doesn't carry over. If you allow your focus to be in the rear-view mirror rather than looking straight at what's in front of you, then what's gone before can be a distraction. We will not allow this. This group of players are all about what's next. And that's how they treat each and every day.

Finally, I wish to use these notes to pay tribute to a person the football community sadly lost last week: Walter Smith.

I had the privilege of meeting Walter on a couple of occasions in his role with the League Managers' Association. I had of course heard of his reputation as a manager prior to us coming together. His record was remarkable.

I am always a big believer that those who know someone best are actually the most interesting to hear from, when it comes to remembering a special life. Andy Robertson's words summed up what he meant to Scottish football, regardless of what generation you are from or which club you support there. But I was really touched by the tributes from Sir Kenny Dalglish, Sir Alex Ferguson and Ally McCoist.

With Walter having worked on Merseyside for Everton, I know there are a lot of people associated with Liverpool who will miss him also. On behalf of the team I send our love and condolences to his family.

To our supporters, I hope they find joy and energy in today's game. They know we will need them, because we always do.

We will try and be at our best and hopefully put in a performance to again make them proud.

Liverpool 2, Brighton 2

Goals: Henderson (4), Mane (24)

Line-up: Alisson, Alexander-Arnold, Konate, Van Dijk, Robertson, Keita (Oxlade-Chamberlain 19), Henderson, Jones (Minamino 87), Salah, Firmino (Jota 78), Mane. Subs not used: Gomez, Adrian, Tsimikas, Origi, Matip, Morton

Jürgen's post-match reaction: 'I cannot change it now, [but] it feels like a defeat even though I know it's not a defeat. It is a deserved point for Brighton, obviously, for different reasons. It's unnecessary because in our good moments we were really good, we showed how you have to play against Brighton but then with not playing enough football anymore, we opened the door for them. The best way to defend Brighton is to have the ball yourself and that's what we didn't do for long enough. That's why we scored the two goals, which were incredible, especially the two goals which were disallowed were incredible. Sadio's second goal was my favourite goal of all six years in Liverpool because of how we put them under pressure there; it was just insane and unlucky with the handball. Then they scored their goal – not sure if it was a cross or not, but who cares because the ball was in – and we didn't play enough football anymore, not the right football. In our good moments, we attacked the centre of Brighton, which is where you have to do it and then we didn't do that anymore. We slowed the game down in the wrong moments, we didn't show enough initiative in other moments and that's then just not good enough. I think after Mo's goal in the second half, which was disallowed, I can't remember a lot [of chances] – maybe in the last four or five minutes we were a bit more on the front foot again, but apart from that we just tried to calm the game down when we had the ball and defended them when they had the ball. They scored a wonderful second goal and that's why they deserve a point.'

NOV

2021

The Reds made light work of a difficult group to qualify for the knock-out stages of the Champions League. A first defeat of the season was suffered but a couple of big wins meant a title challenge was still on the cards

3rd: Atletico Madrid (CL) H
7th: West Ham (PL) A
20th: Arsenal (PL) H
24th: Porto (CL) H
27th: Southampton (PL) H

v Atletico Madrid
Wednesday, November 3rd, 8pm

'WE TREAT EACH MATCH LIKE IT IS A FINAL BUT WE KNOW THE SEASON ITSELF IS A PROCESS'

UEFA Champions League

Jürgen Klopp

GOOD evening and welcome back to Anfield for our UEFA Champions League game against Atletico Madrid. I specifically welcome Diego Simeone, his players, staff, officials and the supporters of our visitors.

Of course it is not that long ago that we faced each other in what was a highly eventful contest and I'm pretty sure a lot of the 'drama' around that game has dominated the build-up.

One of the advantages of having a programme column such as this one is that I can say in a very precise and unedited way what I actually think about certain things.

I want to be as clear as I possibly can that my respect for Diego and his achievements could not be higher. It really couldn't.

I know previous comments from me have probably allowed for a different view to be taken. From the questions I had ahead of the match in Madrid it is clear it is perceived that way by certain people.

Diego Simeone is one of the best coaches and managers in world football and he has been for a sustained period of time. His team is a results machine and ultimately that is what this job is about for those of us privileged to get the chance to do it at a professional level.

He is a competitor and he is a winner. He has managed to re-invent Atletico Madrid a couple of times and yet maintain the principles and direction he and his staff want them to go in.

They are Spanish champions and when I look at their quality, from front to back, I would expect them to retain their crown and rightly be considered one of the favourites for the competition we play in this evening.

They are a top, top team, one of the world's most powerful clubs and they consistently perform well. They have our total respect.

Of course, that respect doesn't mean we temper our own expectations. On the occasions we have faced each other over the past few years I think we have always shown our own quality, including the last match in Madrid.

When you prepare to face them you know you have to win the battle first. You have to be prepared to stand toe-to-toe and fight. If you don't win the fight you have no chance of winning the contest.

But we have always demonstrated we have the ability to do both. We have the steel and resolve that is second to no-one. We cannot be out-fought or out-worked when we are in the right mood. And this set of players are often in the right mood, by the way. I love this about us.

The last time we played each other here, at Anfield, Atletico won the tie but our performance that night was exceptional. Honestly, I have no problem saying it is among my favourites from how we have played in a European game at our home and we've been blessed with some special ones.

You know they will be hungry and determined. So we don't just have to match that, we need to better it. We know they'll be streetwise and ruthless. We have to overcome that. We know they'll give all they have effort-wise from the first whistle to the last. We must work even harder than them.

Honestly, as much as this game is one of the most difficult to prepare for, it is one I relish. It's great for us to have this opportunity. Our players feel exactly the same.

At the time of writing this I have no idea who will be available in terms of the line-up after our weekend Premier League outing but I am certain whichever eleven start will be ready.

The Brighton performance and result didn't match what we would have expected of ourselves. That's okay. It's about how we respond.

There were elements of the game which were very pleasing and others that weren't. We need to take information and learnings from both parts; the good and the not-so-good.

It's so important to remember that a football season is an evolving entity. If you think at this stage of it you are perfect you will achieve nothing.

I don't want us to have too many painful learning experiences but I also must accept that this is the period where development is beneficial as we build our base.

As a group we are always our biggest critic. We are constantly asking where we can be better. Where is the margin for improvement? Identify it. Work on it. Then go act on it. And this is never more important than during a campaign itself. We treat each match like it is a final, but we also know the season itself is a process.

What we have done, in the Premier League, the Champions League and the League Cup so far, is good. It's solid foundations. We are in a good way.

But we are greedy for more and that includes the individual and collective level we can perform at.

It's my job, the job of my staff and of course the players now to take it forward. It's what we have done many times since we were together and I know we are ready to do this again.

Finally, as much as I am not usually someone who likes to look back, it is difficult not to think of the last time this particular fixture took place at Anfield and the impact on all of us.

I said earlier how much I loved how we performed that night. This applies to the supporters as much as anyone. The atmosphere inside our stadium was electric. Every LFC supporter was on their toes. It was a vintage European night display from them for sure.

But it took place against the backdrop of grave uncertainty and anxiety for what was about to happen to this country and the wider world.

I had a feeling that evening would be the last football game played for a bit but I genuinely had no idea the wait to have grounds full again would last 18 long months.

Tonight our home will be full again, as it was on that night. More than anything else this gives me excitement for the game. Because I know the feeling you get when this place is 'on it' is an experience you can never have too much of.

Anfield on a European night is a healthy addiction. Let's give it all we have and find joy in the moment.

Liverpool 2, Atletico Madrid 0

Goals: Jota (13), Mane (21)

Line-up: Alisson, Alexander-Arnold (Phillips 90+4), Matip, Van Dijk, Tsimikas, Henderson, Fabinho (Thiago 58), Oxlade-Chamberlain (Minamino 78), Salah, Jota, Mane (Firmino 46 (Origi 78)). Subs not used: Konate, Adrian, Robertson, Kelleher, N Williams, Morton

Jürgen's post-match reaction: 'If Bobby Firmino wouldn't have gone off with a hamstring injury that would have been much better. But from pretty much all other points of view, it was a good performance, it's an incredible group stage so far. I wouldn't have expected that obviously when I saw the draw – nobody would have expected that. Doing that is pretty special. But for tonight, job done but we all know there are two games to go and we will try everything to win them as well. That's how it is. It is a Champions League game, the next one, is at home, the game after that is at the San Siro and I've never played there, so I'm really excited about that. We will play at home [against Porto] and play real football. Can you imagine we play Porto at home, the crowd is really coming from all over the world to watch the games and then you offer, I don't know, a half-cooked dish. That is pretty not much how it will be. We go for it, we want to win football games, that's all.'

Post-match notes

Despite being in a very tough group, four wins in a row meant the Reds had secured top spot with two games to spare and maintained their unbeaten start to the season.

Sunday, November 7th, 4.30pm
Premier League
West Ham 3, Liverpool 2

Goals: Alexander-Arnold (41), Origi (83)

Line-up: Alisson, Alexander-Arnold, Matip, Van Dijk, Robertson, Henderson, Fabinho (Minamino 80), Oxlade-Chamberlain (Thiago 68), Salah, Jota (Origi 76), Mane. Subs not used: Konate, Tsimikas, Phillips, Kelleher, N Williams, Morton

Jürgen's post-match reaction: 'First half completely in control of the game, anyway 1-0 down because of a set-piece. We scored the equaliser – a wonderful goal – and were really in control and in charge of the game. Obviously West Ham play really good stuff this season but today it was a bit more like the old West Ham – sitting deep, going for set-pieces and counter-attacks. In the first half we didn't let that happen apart from one, I think, set-piece, if I'm 100 per cent right, at least where they scored the goal. Then second half we lost balls in general, we lost more balls than in the first half. They scored from a counter-attack and from a set-piece; the second one was exceptionally well taken and a great, fantastic finish from Zouma. For whatever reason, it looked for me a little bit like we lost patience, it was like we didn't have enough clear-cut chances so we wanted to change the wrong things.'

November 2021

v Arsenal
Saturday, November 20th, 5.30pm

'HARVEY HAS GIVEN ENERGY TO OUR GROUP, EVEN WHILE BEING UNABLE TO CONTRIBUTE ON THE PITCH'

Premier League

Jürgen Klopp

GOOD afternoon and welcome back to Anfield for our Premier League match against Arsenal. I welcome Mikel Arteta, his players, staff, officials and supporters of our visitors.

It's really exciting to see the progress Arsenal are making under Mikel's leadership and it's clear he and his coaches have now instilled a clear identity into the side. They are energetic and adventurous. They have a clear plan. They are an extremely dangerous opponent.

Although I wish them zero luck today, I am pleased for Mikel that he is seeing the fruits of his hard work and enterprise come through on the pitch. I thought that during their difficult stages he handled himself superbly and now Arsenal are getting the benefit of that. They are full of confidence. It will make for a cool game, I think.

For us, we come into today looking forward to the opportunity. Liverpool versus Arsenal at Anfield is a tremendous fixture and one that should fill us with positive anticipation.

I have spoken previously in these pages about the early part of the season being about laying a firm foundation. I think we are still in that phase, although with no 'break' now until January this is where the intensity goes to the next level. We are ready for this.

It's important not to get distracted by the league table or weighed down by any specific result.

During our most successful times together, responding to a setback has always been one of our greatest collective qualities. Maybe sometimes that wasn't seen because results were so consistent, but taking a knock doesn't just mean losing or not winning a game, it's often setbacks within games themselves.

In periods like the one we are about to enter now, resilience will be vital. We are all going to be tested and pushed to our limit. How we react and respond will define the sort of season we can expect. Disappointment is fine, but you cannot dwell. Self-analysis is important, but it should not burden.

Today's game I'm sure will be a perfect case study for what is to come. We should and will go into the match focusing on our own qualities. But in this league, with all opponents being so strong and well-coached, there will be moments where we have to dig in, periods where we have to respond to something not going our way. To have any chance of winning a game like this one, you need to be resilient in body and mind. We will be. I know these players.

An individual who is showing incredible personal resilience in this moment is Harvey Elliott. It filled my heart with joy to see him running on the pitches last week.

Yes, he is still in a very early stage of his recovery and it's important to keep expectation around his return realistic. He is still a long way off being able to train fully with the team, let alone play in a game. But his progress is positive and it's more about how he has responded and how he has attacked his rehab. It's a perfect example of how you should react when facing a setback.

Speaking to our wonderful staff, who are treating and managing his recovery, they have been blown away with the maturity he has shown. It would have been perfectly normal for him to have spells where he felt sorry for himself, but we haven't seen that.

Harvey has continued to give energy to our group, even while being unable to contribute on the pitch. He lights up a room when he walks into it.

The key for Harvey is to build on excellent work he has done until now – a bit like a team laying a foundation for a season. All the positive steps he makes are towards the goal and returning in the best shape possible. He may have bumps and stumbles on the remaining part of his road to recovery, but as long as he reacts in the right way, those moments won't define it.

Speaking about positive feelings, I was really pleased to see so many of our players have successful and joyful experiences while on international duty. As I have spoken about many times – and I'm sure it's the same for Mikel – these breaks are stressful for club managers only because you want your players to return healthy.

It was fantastic to see so many of our squad achieve success with their respective countries last week, by either gaining outright qualification for the next World Cup or securing a play-off spot.

It is such an honour to earn that opportunity and I know for the boys who have it to look forward to next year, it will be a source of focus and motivation. Huge congratulations to the players from both sides who are now qualified. It shouldn't be underestimated that playing at a World Cup is something you earn and achieve, therefore they should feel the pride that comes with that.

Finally, turning back to today, the atmosphere and energy inside Anfield for a Liverpool versus Arsenal fixture has always been one of the best I've experienced since I came to this club. There is always a buzz around this game. I expect nothing less today, given both teams are filled with energetic, positive talent who come into each game with intent.

Since we have been allowed to be together again inside stadiums, our home has been on its toes for each match. We are so appreciative of this. We didn't have too many Anfield games during the last block of fixtures, but this is a period where we go again as a collective.

We will need our supporters more than ever in the coming weeks and months. They are a key factor in us building the resilience we will need to weather the storm of such an intense campaign. Being as knowledgeable as they are, they know their role and will embrace their importance.

Anfield is an energy source that doesn't diminish and we are always grateful for it.

Hopefully we can produce a performance and result to make them proud.

Liverpool 4, Arsenal 0

Goals: Mane (39), Jota (52), Salah (73), Minamino (77)

Line-up: Alisson, Alexander-Arnold, Matip, Van Dijk, Tsimikas, Oxlade-Chamberlain (Henderson 76), Fabinho, Thiago (Morton 84), Salah, Jota (Minamino 76), Mane. Subs not used: Konate, Phillips, Gordon, Kelleher, Beck, Bradley

Jürgen's post-match reaction: 'So we had to show a reaction, that's clear. The only problem that we had was that we were not together most of the time [during the international break]... the boys grew in the game today, which is very important in football – you cannot only play well if you start pretty much with three or four chances in five minutes – and played then good football. We were in control in the beginning but we just were not used to the way Arsenal played today. The boys did really well. We scored the 1-0 and what I didn't like about the first half – and the first half was fine, we had a lot of good moments, we could have done better in some but there was still a lot of good moments – but I didn't like that the best phase of Arsenal was after we scored the 1-0. So you can see these moments, being under pressure slightly, being relieved that we had now scored the one goal, but it's still not right. So we had to change that and we changed and I think after half-time we had a really impressive phase and controlled the game again. It was a mix of a very mature performance and a very exciting [performance], with very, very exciting moments: very exciting goals, great counter-press, great high-press, it was really good. And then finishing the situations off and it's an impressive result, no doubt about that.'

Post-match notes

The Reds got back to winning ways, and in doing so halted Arsenal's 10-match unbeaten run in style. It was Alisson's 50th Premier League clean sheet, making him the 10th Liverpool keeper to reach 50 in league games.

Jürgen Klopp

v Porto
Wednesday, November 24th, 8pm

'THERE IS NO ACCEPTABLE LEVEL OF COMMITMENT THAT FALLS BELOW 100 PER CENT'

UEFA Champions League

November 2021

GOOD evening and welcome back to Anfield for our UEFA Champions League match against FC Porto. I welcome Sérgio Conceição, his players and staff, as well as the officials and supporters of our visitors.

We have faced each other on a number of occasions in recent years and the respect I have for Sérgio as a coach and leader could not be higher. They are an outstandingly well-organised team, who are streetwise and technically very gifted.

Admittedly the scoreline of the previous games suggest we have had the ascendancy, but how the matches played out away from the scoreboard tells a different story.

It's always been ultra-competitive and the only reason we have enjoyed good results is because we have shown respect to their quality and looked to win the battle before we could win the game.

Sérgio has been at Porto for a long time now by modern football management standards, which shows how highly they regard him. He is so competitive and I think tonight we will face a really dangerous and hungry opponent. This is cool, because we are just as determined. And I'm sure this will have been the theme of the coverage coming into the contest. Where will our focus be, given our position within the group? I can answer that categorically; we are in this match 100 per cent. We are in it with all we have.

Firstly, it is not possible to represent Liverpool Football Club and go into any game without total commitment. It's just not allowed. The notion that we would treat a game in the Champions League, a competition we cherish so dearly, as anything other than totally meaningful is also not possible to comprehend.

I'm sure there will have been talk about the responsibility we have to the tournament itself, given the group standing and the implications for clubs competing for qualification. But it's not really about that. It's the responsibility we have to ourselves, as professionals and also to our club.

As individuals and as a team, who are blessed to operate at the highest level of this game, we cannot turn on or off a switch whereby we see a game mattering less because of what a group table looks like.

There is no acceptable level of commitment that falls below 100 per cent when doing this job. My players and staff know this. We do not need reminding.

Of course we will have to make sensible decisions as regards our team selection. At the time of writing this column I have no idea who will and won't be available, but given the intensity of the schedule we have it is inevitable we will need to make use of our brilliant squad over this period. That would have been the case regardless of our current qualification status.

We have so many players at the moment who are, on

a daily basis on the training pitches, earning the right to play in this wonderful team. I could pick out a number of examples, but I would like to highlight Takumi Minamino.

Taki scored for us at the weekend after being on the pitch for a matter of seconds and I promise you there will not have been a more popular goalscorer in our group at that moment. You could tell that from all of our reactions.

This is, of course, partly because we love him as a person. He has such a warm and generous soul. However, it was far more than just his endearing personality that made us so pleased. It was because of the attitude he shows and the contribution he makes day-in and day-out.

Without question he is a person who helps set our standards. I cannot praise highly enough the level he shows in training. He takes the maximum possible from each session. He is a coach's dream.

Being ready to contribute is a prerequisite for being a member of our group. Taki has been the epitome of it this season, along with others, and it will be an important quality for us going forward.

The other individual I want to mention following the weekend's action against Arsenal is Tyler Morton. It would not have been lost on our supporters that our bench that day had a fair share of youthfulness about it.

I heard all the 'past their bedtime' jokes. Tyler came on and the image of him being embraced by Thiago as he entered the pitch was really quite something.

Tyler represents everything that is great about young footballers at our club. I know how highly Alex Inglethorpe and the Academy staff rate him. What a job they continue to do.

He doesn't need any more expectation placed on him, so I am not going to write a 'love song' here about what he is going to do in the game or what sort of player he is and might be. We will see on that and he will write his own story. But it is the person he is that makes him very special.

He earned those Premier League minutes and in doing so set an example to the young players who will inevitably follow him. He is such a credit to himself and his family. His job now is to continue to lean into the best personal qualities that have helped him to this point. That is all: be the same guy who treats each second with the first team as an opportunity to learn and be better.

And it is on that theme that I want to finish this particular column. Within my first-team staff we have a coach who is the ultimate champion of players like Tyler. He is the reason these young lads can transition into our environment so well. It's why they can be ready.

Vitor Matos joined our club a few years ago now and I feel blessed every day that we made that decision. Of course, he came to us from FC Porto and it is a club and a place very dear to him. I know he still has many great friends there.

He is one of the smartest people I have been lucky enough to work with and he is consumed with coaching and developing players at all levels. Our more senior guys will testify to the contribution he makes to them also.

Portugal has long been a breeding ground for some of the brightest coaching talent in world football and Vitor absolutely belongs on any list of that next generation of stars. Fortunately for us he loves working here and we can benefit from his skills for the foreseeable future.

I hope we can all enjoy this match this evening. It's a Champions League game under the lights at Anfield. It's all the billing any contest should need. Our supporters know we will need them. We always do.

Liverpool 2, Porto 0

Goals: Thiago (52), Salah (70)

Line-up: Alisson, N Williams, Matip, Konate, Tsimikas (Robertson 63), Oxlade-Chamberlain (Milner 82), Morton, Thiago (Henderson 63), Salah (Fabinho 71), Minamino, Mane (Origi 72). Subs not used: Van Dijk, Adrian, Jota, Phillips, Kelleher, Alexander-Arnold

Jürgen's post-match reaction: 'We could have lost this game tonight. We gave chances away where they could have scored and that would have made the game obviously really difficult, so we should not make too much of it. We were lucky in moments. But yes, we have our moments where we are really not cool to play against, that's true. And I didn't expect that tonight really because we changed decisive things, to be honest, and you don't expect then the boys immediately get like a ruthless pressing machine or whatever. You just know we have to grow into the game and that's happened actually – that's what I'm happy about. Whoever sees Thiago in training knows he has the technique to do it [score a wonderful goal], but even with this technique it doesn't happen constantly that he can fire such a thunderball. It was good timing, to be honest. Great goal.'

Post-match notes

Mo Salah took his tally to 17 goals in 17 games this season but Thiago's sweet strike from 30 yards was the highlight of the match. The Reds became the first team since Wolves in 1939 to score two or more goals in 16 consecutive matches. Tyler Morton made his first Champions League start while Porto have failed to beat the Reds in any of their 10 meetings.

November 2021

v Southampton
Saturday, November 27th, 3pm

'LIFE IS MORE FUN WHEN YOU ARE TOLERANT AND INCLUSIVE. THOSE WHO AREN'T ARE MISSING OUT'

Premier League

GOOD afternoon and welcome back to Anfield for our Premier League game against Southampton. I welcome Ralph Hasenhüttl, his players, staff, officials and supporters of the visitors.

It's pretty well-known that I think Ralph is a top manager and a really cool guy. He's someone whom I enjoy speaking to and whose approach to football I really admire. Courageous coach with a clear idea. A proper leader. I think Southampton are very fortunate to have him and I know that feeling is reciprocated.

A match against Ralph's Southampton always means one thing: you are in for a fight. We have seen this in previous seasons and I know for a fact we will see it today.

They have had a full week to prepare, while we, of course, were in European action only on Wednesday.

I am writing this column prior to the game against Porto taking place therefore cannot offer any analysis of how that played out. But it is a factor for us and one we must contend with. We are used to this meanwhile so it's all good. Not an issue, just information.

This period is a proper test but one we enjoy, players and staff! It's a test both physically and mentally. As coaches it means we have to be completely focused on preparation for the next game almost the second the full-time whistle goes on the previous one.

I hope I say this a lot, I think I do, but in these moments

I could not appreciate the amazing support staff I have around me more. And not just the immediate coaching staff or the ones visible who sit with me in the dugout on game-day. The wider team behind the team – the guys whose shoulders we stand on.

So much planning goes into making sure we can prepare for each game like it is the most important one we will ever play. The energy and commitment to making sure everything in our environment is perfect for elite performance has to be seen to be appreciated. I see it every day at the AXA Training Centre and I appreciate it like crazy.

We know how privileged we are to do what we do and that so many would give anything to swap places with us and have our experiences. But it doesn't mean that the many dedicated staff who perform the duties day in and day out, don't feel the strain at certain times. The intensity of the schedule affects them also, but unlike the players, myself and my most senior coaching staff, they rarely get the public plaudits.

What they do in this moment creates a base for the team to flourish. We are so lucky to have them.

Hopefully it won't have escaped anyone's attention that today we highlight the Rainbow Laces campaign. This season it is known as 'Lace Up and Speak Up'!

Each year it feels like it gets more prominent and this is important. It is clearly an area in which we as a game, particularly on the men's side, have far more to do before we can consider it a truly welcoming and inclusive environment for members of the LGBT+ community.

I have to be honest, there are times when I personally am guilty of complacency with this issue in particular because to me it is just so normal that people should feel safe to be exactly who they are, free from judgement or prejudice.

I honestly believe that in the team itself, in this country certainly but also Germany and others, it would be absolutely welcomed. Hand on heart, I think players throughout the professional men's game would think: cool, delighted you can be yourself, this is how it should be…now let's work!

But me saying that and believing that is one thing. The fact that in men's professional football in the biggest leagues there are no openly gay players means we have more to do and campaigns like this matter so much.

I was lucky to spend some time with Meikayla Moore from the LFC Women's team in the build-up to today. It was to create a video for our supporters which would help raise awareness. What an incredible person Meikayla is. Inspirational.

And I learned from her. I am 54 and I think and I hope a well-educated person on these matters, but she still told me things which opened my eyes and opened my mind. Listening to her was important for me. It broadened by understanding even further.

This is how we really make the progress whereby those who play and those who support will truly feel free and comfortable to be exactly who they are while being in our game, be it dressing room or the terraces. Fully-included, no worry or anxiety to hide their true selves because football has a closed mind.

I hope all our fans take the opportunity around this fixture to research and look up some of the great work being done in this area. You're never too old to improve yourself, I've learned that. Life is more fun when you are tolerant and inclusive. It's those who aren't who are missing out.

Today as a club and a family of fans we also celebrate the LFC Foundation Community Day, which is an opportunity to showcase all the great work that the charity does both in the local community and around the world.

I am proud to be an ambassador of LFC Foundation and I have seen first-hand the incredible impact that their work has on young people and their families.

Without the unwavering support of the Liverpool FC family this important work would not be possible, so from everyone at the club, thank you for the generosity and kindness you have shown and I know you will continue to show.

Very finally, it's our third home game this week and therefore our third opportunity for Anfield to do its thing. We need Anfield – in fact today we will really need Anfield. We need Anfield to show its best face. I'm sure it will, it never lets us down.

Liverpool 4, Southampton 0

Goals: Jota (2, 32), Thiago (37), Van Dijk (52)

Line-up: Alisson, Alexander-Arnold, Konate, Van Dijk, Robertson, Henderson (Milner 67), Fabinho, Thiago (Oxlade-Chamberlain 59), Salah, Jota (Minamino 81), Mane. Subs not used: Tsimikas, Origi, Matip, Kelleher, N Williams, Morton

Jürgen's post-match reaction: 'Diogo is an exceptional player, exceptional boy. It was a perfect signing because he has everything that a Liverpool player in this squad needs. He has the technical skills, he has the physical skills and he is very smart and can learn all the tactical stuff pretty quick. On top of that, he can play all three positions; in a 4-2-3-1 he could play as the 10. So, it is very helpful. He has the speed, has the desire to finish situations off really good. I think his goalscoring record is pretty impressive. Unfortunately, he had a big injury last year and that is never helpful. But he is back, thank God, and fits really well in this team. I'm really happy for him. Actually, today I thought he could have made a slightly better decision before he then scored, maybe he was smart enough to wait for the next ball that he could finish it off easier. But all good and Diogo is a good player.'

DEC

2021

A busy month included a dramatic late win at Wolves, a penalty shoot-out success in the Carabao Cup and a derby victory that is as comfortable as anything the Reds have experienced at Goodison Park

1st: Everton (PL) A
4th: Wolverhampton W (PL) A
7th: AC Milan (CL) A
11th: Aston Villa (PL) H
16th: Newcastle United (PL) H
19th: Tottenham (PL) A
22nd: Leicester City (CC) H
28th: Leicester City (PL) A

Wednesday, December 1st, 8.15pm
Premier League
Everton 1, Liverpool 4

Goals: Henderson (9), Salah (19, 64), Jota (79)

Line-up: Alisson, Alexander-Arnold, Matip, Van Dijk, Robertson, Henderson (Oxlade-Chamberlain 83), Fabinho, Thiago (Milner 75), Salah, Jota (Minamino 88), Mane. Subs not used: Konate, Tsimikas, Origi, Kelleher, N Williams, Morton

Jürgen's post-match reaction: 'It was, for sure, the best performance we've shown since I'm at Liverpool at Goodison. We had some good games here, but we were never as good as tonight. We were never as calm as tonight, we were never as convinced as tonight and that's why we won the game and I am really happy about that. The two derbies for us against Everton and United are big games and you have to learn to keep yourself calm and together, if you want, to play your best football. I wanted us today to be really mature and, yes, very aggressive but in a football way, angry as well but in a football way.'

Post-match notes

In scoring four goals at Goodison Park it meant the Reds had scored two or more goals in 18 successive matches. It was the Reds' biggest win at Everton since the Ian Rush-inspired 5-0 win in 1982.

Saturday, December 4th, 3pm
Premier League
Wolverhampton W 0, Liverpool 1

Goal: Origi (90+4)

Line-up: Alisson, Alexander-Arnold, Matip, Van Dijk, Robertson, Henderson (Origi 68), Fabinho, Thiago, Salah (Milner 90+6), Jota (Oxlade-Chamberlain 82), Mane. Subs not used: Konate, Minamino, Tsimikas, Phillips, Kelleher, N Williams

Jürgen's post-match reaction: 'It's really important and feels really big today for us, to be honest, because it was a very difficult game. The wind makes football really difficult and today, especially for the dominant side. We missed a lot of chances and we had to defend the counter-attacks of Wolves. That was the challenge. It was clear: when you don't score you just have to keep going and that's what we did. And then Divock Origi, the legend, came and finished it off for us. I love it. I think a point would have been lucky for Wolves, so it's the right result.'

Post-match notes

Divock Origi's late strike was the 13th time the Reds had scored after 90 minutes to win a game since Jürgen Klopp became Liverpool manager – at least four more than any other team in the same time.

Tuesday, December 7th, 8pm
UEFA Champions League
AC Milan 1, Liverpool 2

Goals: Salah (36), Origi (55)

Line-up: Alisson, N Williams (Bradley 90+3), Phillips, Konate, Tsimikas, Oxlade-Chamberlain, Morton, Minamino (Woltman 90+3), Salah (Keita 64), Origi (Fabinho 80), Mane (Gomez 64). Subs not used: Robertson, Matip, Dixon-Bonner, Kelleher, Alexander-Arnold, Norris, Davies

Jürgen's post-match reaction: 'I don't feel pride a lot in football because most of the time I expect good things, but tonight fills me with a lot of pride. It's an exceptional performance. I don't mean that we won six games – the reason is especially this game because it was so good. It is easy for me to make the changes but the boys have to then be confident enough to show how good they are. The fact we won all the games, which is incredible, is just another chapter in the history of this wonderful group of players.'

Post-match notes

Liverpool became the first English team to win all six Champions League group games in one campaign. Mo Salah's goal meant he became the first Liverpool player since Ian Rush to score 20 or more in five successive seasons. Divock Origi's winner was his first Champions League goal since his strike in the 2019 final.

v Aston Villa
Saturday, December 11th, 3pm

'STEVEN HAS ALWAYS HAD FOCUS ON ONE THING: WINNING'

Premier League

GOOD afternoon and welcome back to Anfield for our Premier League fixture against Aston Villa. I welcome Steven Gerrard, his players and staff and also the officials and supporters of our visitors.

There will be no person inside this stadium today more keen to keep the focus entirely on the match itself than Steven. This is a tough column to write in many respects, because of course it is important to acknowledge what a significant moment it is, having him return today, but at the same time not lose sight of the fact that for 90 minutes we are opponents.

It's fantastic news for the Premier League to have Steven Gerrard in our competition as a manager. Typical of him, he has done everything properly on his path to such a terrific club like Villa.

I remember the discussion we had when it was very early in his coaching career and we talked about the most suitable role at LFC for that to begin. Stevie chose a tough route. He didn't want shortcuts. Speak to our Academy staff and they'll tell you he was a guy who didn't want his previous status within the club to count for anything when he started.

He wanted to be judged on the work he did as a coach and Under-18s manager. I can't begin to tell you how much respect I had for him in how he went about that.

And then, his first senior job was far from being a holiday. The expectation and history of a great club like

Rangers could have been difficult for a lesser leader, but he made them better each season and eventually he made them champions.

Steven is the professional he is and has had the career he has had, until now, because he has always had focus on one thing: winning!

He doesn't come here today for any sentiment or nostalgia. He comes to win. He comes to beat us. This is how it should be and we must be ready.

Of course, there will be an opportunity for our supporters to show love, respect and affection for a person who is rightly considered one of the all-time greats to ever wear a Liverpool shirt. But that is completely separate to the game.

Steven is a serious guy. His commitment to Aston Villa today is absolute. They will be an extremely dangerous opponent who are full of confidence and in good form and we have to be ready.

We too are in a good moment, but we are in it because our players avoid distraction and keep tunnel-vision on performance in the next game only.

Tuesday night in Milan was very pleasing and to progress through such a tough group with a 100 per cent record made me very proud of my players. But it was evident after how quickly the team drew a line. We know we cannot take any of that through with us when the knockout stages start, so we don't dwell.

We are satisfied that we achieved an objective – qualification to the next stage – but that is all for now.

It is exactly the same with our domestic focus. We have had some nice moments in recent weeks and we enjoyed them at the time, but they too must be boxed off.

Aston Villa is such a strong team and we cannot have our minds on anything today other than winning individual and collective battles during the 90 minutes plus stoppage-time. Stay totally in the game. Know there will be setbacks within the contest itself and be ready to respond. Know that today the only thing that can be won is three points, so let's try with all we have to achieve that.

This squad has shown they all recognise the value of their contribution, and for us to enjoy great moments every single person has to perform to their best each and every day. I can't begin to tell you how valuable that is, to have players who recognise it and embrace it.

I know our supporters enjoyed the footage of the reaction on the bench to our winning goal at Wolves, seeing players who didn't get on the pitch that day celebrate as wildly as those who did. I totally understand why fans love those scenes so much. But that really is just a tiny snapshot of the mentality and togetherness our group has.

More importantly than how they celebrate is how

they approach their work on a daily basis, how they train and keep themselves ready to perform when called upon. I can tell you, until now, it is one of the best I have experienced.

We are in the most intense period of the campaign and it's a period that lasts for weeks and weeks. We are nothing and will achieve nothing without the total commitment of this entire playing squad. We are so blessed, as a club, to have this remarkable group of players who put collective achievement above all else. It must stay this way and we will all work to make it so.

Anyone who reads these programme notes regularly will know that I don't need a second invitation to praise our wonderful fans. The support they give is second to none and I will always be grateful for this. You only have to look at how many travelled to Milan in midweek even though we had already qualified and despite the travelling restrictions that we all have to endure to know how special our supporters are.

But if a good relationship is built on honesty, there is a concern that I have to raise about a problem that has crept in recently. In quite a few games we have had supporters run on the pitch and this is something that needs to stop.

As a club, we have worked incredibly hard to build a special bond between players and supporters and in the right circumstances I want the interaction between both to be at the highest level. I want the players to know how lucky they are to play for this club and for our supporters, and I want our supporters to know that the players are playing for them.

The more we can be together, the better – but the pitch itself is an exception to this. We are still in the midst of a pandemic and this means the players spend their times in red zones, doing everything they can to limit contact so that games can be played.

This precaution is absolutely necessary but it means the players have to make sacrifices in their own lives in order to reduce the risk of infection. The pitch is a red zone and needs to be treated that way.

But even if these measures were not needed, safety and security would still be a priority. The safety of our supporters and our players is always paramount and we know that this is jeopardised whenever anyone enters the playing area who isn't supposed to be there.

At Everton last week, a steward fell awkwardly when he tried to stop someone from running on the pitch. Shortly after, Alisson had to take evasive action to avoid another supporter who almost knocked him over. It was not so long ago that Adrian was injured by a pitch invader who caught him by accident as we celebrated winning the Super Cup in Istanbul. None of these outcomes or risks are worthwhile.

Whenever we win games I want to celebrate with our

supporters but our ability to do so is undermined if we have security issues. This was the case at Goodison where I would have loved to have spent longer enjoying the moment with our fans but it just was not possible because the stewards had to clear the pitch.

This isn't the way we want it to be. We want to share special times with you, but the best way of doing this is by all of us being in the place that we're supposed to be. Anything else doesn't make sense.

So finally – and it's back to where I started this column – we all have a game to focus on today and we must all be on our toes.

The management, players and fans of Aston Villa mean business. We can't just look to match what they bring, that won't be enough – we must try with all we have to be better.

We will need the unique energy Anfield brings. We will need every person inside our stadium to give our players extra spring, extra bounce, extra power.

It's such an exciting fixture and one I really can't wait to see play out.

As always thank you for your amazing support and we will look to make you proud with our effort and performance.

Liverpool 1, Aston Villa 0

Goal: Salah (67pen)

Line-up: Alisson, Alexander-Arnold, Matip, Van Dijk, Robertson, Henderson, Fabinho, Thiago (Milner 83), Salah, Oxlade-Chamberlain (Jota 58), Mane (Minamino 88). Subs not used: Konate, Keita, Gomez, Tsimikas, Kelleher, N Williams

Jürgen's post-match reaction: 'It's difficult for us to really work on it [keeping clean sheets] because our problem is that we obviously play all the time. If this squad, this team defends on the highest level we always have a chance to score a goal and if we don't do that then we need to score two, three, four or whatever and that makes no sense because that's not always possible. The most important thing is that you are well protected because then you feel really free for offensive things. I am really happy with that, but the last 15 minutes today I am not happy with, of course. How could I [be] because we really opened the door, but the 75 before were outstanding so I'm really happy about the performance. Around the games we are both [Jürgen and Steven Gerrard] pretty focused. That's the idea of this game, that you can be the best friend with somebody and when you play against each other you want to beat him. The whole fuss around it was absolutely right but there is one person it was not so easy [for] and that's Stevie. He is a Liverpool legend. They did really well, they obviously fought really hard for a result here today, pushed by Stevie.'

Post-match notes

Steven Gerrard returned to Anfield as a manager for the first time. It was Liverpool's 100th 1-0 Premier League win.

December 2021

v Newcastle United
Thursday, December 16th, 8pm

'IT'S A GAME THAT GETS JUICES FLOWING ON BOTH SIDES. THIS IS COOL'

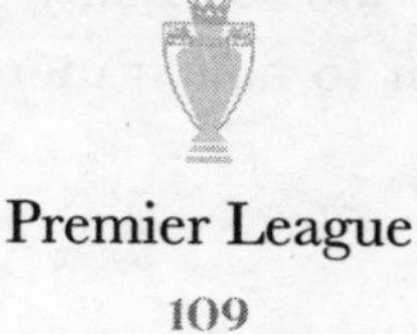

Premier League

GOOD evening and welcome back to Anfield for our Premier League fixture against Newcastle United. I welcome Eddie Howe, his players, staff, officials and the supporters of our visitors.

It really is great to see Eddie back in management and back in the Premier League. I've never hidden my admiration for him and his work.

He is a brave, adventurous coach with a clear plan and a clear idea, always. What he did at Bournemouth you could make a movie about, it was such a remarkable story.

I am guessing this, but I think the break will have helped him and made him even better. A time to take a breather, reflect and learn more; refine new ideas.

Judging from how he has presented himself in the media, he is full of energy for this new role and excited about the potential at Newcastle.

I know from previous experiences his side will come to Anfield and look to attack us. Get at us. Play their game. We need to be ready. They have an excellent squad of players who have a lot to fight for. They will be a dangerous opponent for sure.

There is one person in their camp whom we at LFC know particularly well. Mark Leyland was a key member of my backroom team for many years as an analyst but has recently left to take a more senior position at Newcastle.

He had worked with Eddie previously at Burnley, I believe, and as disappointed as we all are to lose Mark, it's not a surprise Eddie and his guys wanted him and it's a fantastic opportunity.

He is a really smart guy, wonderfully generous with a warm personality. A credit to his superb family, Newcastle are very fortunate to have him.

We gave him a round of applause at the AXA Training Centre on his last day but it's worked out that I can use this programme column to thank Mark again for all he did for me and the team in the time we spent together. I wish him all the luck in the world for the future but none at all today of course.

At the time of writing this column I have no idea what impact the previous game against Aston Villa will have had on team selection. There is, of course, a wider national conversation on the increasing spread of COVID, both in the country but at football clubs also.

My message around this has always been simple and clear, I hope: I trust experts. I follow the advice of smart, educated people who know their field because they've dedicated their lives to it and have studied it.

We are clearly moving back to stricter measures around the team environment and at LFC we are absolutely okay with that.

As I have spoken about before, we have a very high take-up of the vaccine at our club and have done for a long time. It might be 100 per cent now or as close as is possible, so that's important.

I have no issue telling you I received my booster jab as soon as I was eligible and again that will be the case for many, if not nearly all, within our ranks in the coming days and weeks.

I won't apologise for the view I hold on the vaccination, no matter how unpopular it might make me in certain sections of society. I'm the same privately as I am publicly on this.

If I come across friends or people I care about in my life away from football and they tell me they haven't had a jab yet, I do my best to encourage them to listen to experts. It's never a case of 'listen to me' – it's always 'listen to those who know'.

Ignore those who pretend to know. Ignore lies and misinformation. Listen to people who know best. If you do that, you end up wanting the vaccine and the booster.

The 'stick to football' abuse so misses the point. Yes, I know about football having spent my entire life in the game. And my view on the vaccination isn't from my own imagination. That's the point – I listen to experts. People who are smarter than I ever could be, have come to the rescue of society by creating this for the world.

We are very blessed in this country and throughout Europe to have such incredible access to it. I see that as a privilege and one I will always be grateful for. We don't know what impact the new variant will have on football in the short or medium term. It will certainly impact player availability as positive cases arise and might result in fixtures being postponed sporadically, but that is for the governing bodies to manage.

Clearly we hope disruption is minimal, but that's not in our hands and nor should it be. Again, we must trust those who know best, those with the knowledge. We just want as many people as possible to be safe.

Health has to be the priority always. Health of participants, staff and supporters.

Turning back to tonight, the impact of the supporters will be crucial. Anfield was outstanding against Aston Villa. Absolutely outstanding. Player of the match really! It's even more important tonight that we all go again in the same mood.

We need to be focused, controlled, patient but ultimately greedy and channelling positive aggression. The right sort of greed and aggression. The intensity of the backing from the stands on Saturday 100 per cent made a difference and the players responded.

I realise meanwhile Liverpool v Newcastle at Anfield is a fixture that brings romanticism because of rivalries past and when it comes around it's a game that gets the juices flowing on both sides. This is cool.

We can all embrace this feeling tonight. Being back

together, knowing that we can achieve something by helping each other and focusing on what helps us collectively.

When this team and Anfield are in the right mood I always love what we create. The same again would be fantastic.

Hopefully we can perform to make the supporters proud.

Liverpool 3, Newcastle United 1

Goals: Jota (21), Salah (25), Alexander-Arnold (87)

Line-up: Alisson, Alexander-Arnold, Matip, Konate, Robertson, Oxlade-Chamberlain (Keita 74), Henderson, Thiago (Milner 90), Salah (Firmino 74), Jota, Mane. Subs not used: Gomez, Minamino, Tsimikas, Kelleher, N Williams, Pitaluga

Jürgen's post-match reaction: 'The opponent is obviously fighting for staying in the league, put everything in, threw everything on the pitch, had a very defensive organisation, went 1-0 up – so this is the recipe for a difficult game. But we still won it – absolutely deserved and that's it pretty much.'

Post-match notes

This was Liverpool's 2,000th win in the top flight. A goal from Mo Salah meant he equalled Jamie Vardy's Premier League record of scoring or assisting in 15 consecutive games.

December 2021

Sunday, December 19th, 4.30pm
Premier League
Tottenham 2, Liverpool 2

Goals: Jota (35), Robertson (69)

Line-up: Alisson, Alexander-Arnold, Matip, Konate, Robertson, Keita, Morton (Firmino 60), Milner, Salah, Jota (Gomez 90+2), Mane (Tsimikas 82). Subs not used: Oxlade-Chamberlain, Minamino, Gordon, Kelleher, N Williams, Quansah

Jürgen's post-match reaction: 'The result is fine, would've been different, I think, with different decisions from the ref. But with the decisions, how he did it, I'm fine with the result. It's a 2-2 at Tottenham – that's absolutely okay. It was a difficult game for us for plenty of reasons. One is that we had to change a lot and it's obviously then difficult to deal with the different challenges in a game like this. The challenge was today we play against Tottenham, who set up a 5-3-2 and when they won the ball deep in their own half, they just kicked it as far as possible and Kane and Son were on their bikes for it, so we struggled with these moments slightly. It costs you obviously, it gives you some struggles a little bit, so we had to reorganise our protection a little bit better in the second half. It was an intense game, Tottenham looked second half slightly fresher than us. Yeah, we were 2-1 up, they couldn't score the second as well. But, of course, the game would have been completely different with two key decisions in the first half. As for Robbo's red card, we saw it now back and, yes, you can give a red card there. It's not the harshest ever but it's not the smartest as well. He knows that and he's a really good boy but he lost it a little bit, so this red card you can give. But this is the proof that the VAR was there today because before that we thought he might not be in his office, because the two other situations I think we all agree now that Harry Kane should have seen a red card and he didn't. And the penalty situation, Mr Tierney told me that he thought Diogo Jota stopped on purpose, he wanted to get hit. If you watch this situation back, that's a very exclusive view and it's really difficult to do these things that quick. It was a very quick decision of him – you could see that he saw it and was directly like this. I'm not sure if he was prepared for it or whatever but if you watch the situation, how can you react that quick? It's a clear penalty but he thought it's clearly not a penalty. Wow. That's obviously two wrong decisions of him, I would say, and one right – all three against us.'

Post-match notes

With several big names missing due to Covid and other illness, Tyler Morton made his first Premier League start. The 19-year-old was only 10 days old when midfield partner James Milner made his league debut in 2002. In their 18th Premier League match of the season, the Reds reached 50 goals – the fewest number of games they have taken to reach that landmark.

December 2021

v Leicester City
Wednesday, December 22nd, 7.45pm

'LET'S MAKE SURE WE HELP ANYONE WHO FEELS LIKE THEY ARE WALKING ALONE'

Carabao Cup fifth round

Jürgen Klopp

GOOD evening and welcome to Anfield for our Carabao Cup match against Leicester City. I welcome Brendan Rodgers, his players, staff, officials and the supporters of our visitors.

When Brendan returns here he does so, of course, as an opponent but also as a great friend of our club. A friendship based on shared past experiences and fellowship. A friendship from LFC's side based on gratitude for his huge contribution to the progress this club has made in the past decade.

All that said, the friendship is paused for the 90 minutes – that much is clear for both sides.

Leicester, under Brendan, are again one of the most adventurous and exciting sides in our league. Honestly, I love watching them play. Less so having to play against them.

Winning the FA Cup last season was a brilliant collective achievement for Leicester of course. But for Brendan and his staff, I could not have been more pleased for them.

Brendan enjoyed incredible success in Scotland with Celtic. Their dominance under him was frightening. I think consolidating that by winning a trophy in England also is a big statement. Their performance in the final outlined why, under Brendan, they are the real deal to consistently challenge for honours.

They are the complete package. An excellent squad

of players with great balance and who are developing season-on-season. They have new training facilities to go with a ground that is always full and passionately behind them. And an outstanding football leader in Brendan. Cool mix.

Tonight, though, we are rivals and we desperately want to end their participation in this cup competition. There is a semi-final place up for grabs. We want it and so do they. So let's go. Game on.

Of course it is not possible to write this column without acknowledging the growing anxiety in society and football around the COVID situation. Since I last wrote in this programme we have had confirmed cases ourselves within our group. These have been publicised. That we have these cases is not cool and as a human being it does cause worry.

It is difficult for everyone with the uncertainty around. That does inevitably cause concern.

I am now going to repeat myself, but I think we have to keep going until we are told it is not safe or right to do so any more. Trust me, if or when that moment comes we will follow what we are told is right for the health and well-being of everyone. We wouldn't challenge it for one second.

As of this moment, writing this, that hasn't happened yet. The process for us last week, after learning of players recording positive test results, was to inform the

Premier League and wait for guidance and instruction.

Ahead of Tottenham away in particular we were in communication with the league, via their medical advisory guys, and it was apparent that postponement of the game wouldn't have been something they would consider given the level of infection within our group. So, we follow that guidance and we play.

We play until we are told we should stop. We have to trust those making the decisions.

I do passionately believe we have to look at the schedule as part of this though. My view on the lack of recovery and preparation time for players over this period is well documented.

This, though, is different. Even though I don't think it is right in normal times, it feels wrong to insist teams play fixtures within two days of each other in this present situation.

Every squad will have been impacted by the current COVID crisis in some way, clearly some more than others. But we cannot put our hands over our eyes and pretend this is a 'normal' situation. It isn't. It's extraordinary. And on that basis I implore those with the power to make change to intervene.

Please do so for the welfare of the players. It's nothing to do with competition or advantage. To think that in the present climate you would need to be pretty craven.

Look at the situation. Look at the physical strain on

the athletes already. Let's work collaboratively to find a solution. It is not okay to ask teams to play twice in two days at the moment. It is absolutely not okay, actually. It would be entirely wrong. Someone has to act.

I always like to conclude these columns by addressing the supporters directly. I'm not someone who is often lost for words but at the moment it's a struggle to think of the right words.

There is not much I can say that brings encouragement or comfort. I know each household will have its own issues to contend with at this moment.

There'll be people here tonight and reading this gripped with worry about what might happen in the coming days and weeks.

Our supporter-base reflects society. We'll have fans who work for the health service and are about to put themselves in harm's way again and again for the benefit of the rest of us. Likewise other essential workers and the emergency services.

We'll have fans who will be isolating this Christmas, unable to spend time with friends and loved ones. We'll have fans frightened about the impact on their jobs and livelihoods. We'll have fans dealing with the grief of losing loved ones. We'll have fans with various difficulties in their lives which the current situation exacerbates and amplifies to a point it might feel at times unbearable.

What can I say in these circumstances that isn't reductive or insensitive to things that really matter?

I suppose it's this: the common connection we all share is LFC. And via that link, we are family. We are a community.

I send you all my love and my best wishes, as part of my extended family. I send hope that things will get better and we will still be together in this amazing place more often again in the future, immediate or otherwise.

This time of year means different things to different people, those with certain beliefs and those with none at all. But I think what unites all of us around this period is our collective sense of community. Expressing love and care for other people. That's what Christmas means to me. And the current situation strengthens those feelings if I'm being honest.

Please prioritise looking after yourselves and each other. That's my team talk for the LFC family. The best gift you can give your community is to protect each other in times when it's most needed. That is certainly the situation right now.

If it is within our ability to do so, let's make sure we help anyone who feels like they are walking alone. All my love and best wishes.

Liverpool 3, Leicester City 3

(Liverpool win 5-4 on penalties)

Goals: Oxlade-Chamberlain (19), Jota (68), Minamino (90+5)

Line-up: Kelleher, Bradley (Jota 46), Gomez, Koumetio (Konate 46), Tsimikas (Beck 80), Henderson (Keita 59), Morton (Milner 46), Oxlade-Chamberlain, N Williams, Firmino, Minamino. Subs not used: Gordon, Quansah, Woltman, Pitaluga

Jürgen's post-match reaction: 'I don't know the exact percentage of how much we mean to Liverpool supporters in comparison to other things in their lives, but it's a big one. We feel the responsibility but we feel the push we get from them much more. This club is so special. Everything we do is very important. We see it as an advantage that people are so behind us and I love it so much. It's unbelievable. Honestly, if I would have known how good this club is and how much we mean to each other, I would have wanted to be here much earlier. It's absolutely outstanding. I'm really, really happy with the performance, the spirit, with the mentality, in a lot of moments with the football. It was difficult for us in the first half. We had to make a lot of changes [at half-time] and all those changes had reasons and they helped. The boys were outstanding and Caoimhin [Kelleher] in some moments saved our lives. So we are in the semis and that's great.'

Post-match notes

A penalty shoot-out victory put the Reds in their first League Cup semi-final since 2017. James Milner, Bobby Firmino, Alex Oxlade-Chamberlain, Naby Keita and Diogo Jota were the successful takers.

Tuesday, December 28th, 8pm
Premier League
Leicester City 1, Liverpool 0

Line-up: Alisson, Alexander-Arnold, Matip, Van Dijk, Tsimikas, Henderson (Firmino 70), Fabinho (Milner 64), Oxlade-Chamberlain (Keita 55), Salah, Jota, Mane. Subs not used: Konate, Gomez, Jones, Kelleher, Beck, N Williams

Jürgen's post-match reaction: 'We were just not really ourselves tonight. So, we started okay. I didn't like 100 per cent the intensity even in the beginning, but sometimes you have starts like this. But then we lost rhythm and never found it really back. They scored the goal, it was clear we were under pressure, a great atmosphere. We were pushing then but didn't use the chances, missed three headers, all these kinds of things. In the end, what I told everybody who was responsible for the Leicester performance tonight: well deserved.'

Post-match notes

Mo Salah missed a penalty as Liverpool failed to score in a match for the first time this season.

JAN

2022

Despite COVID issues and three star players spending several weeks in Africa representing their nations, the Reds chalked up an unbeaten month that included progress in the FA Cup and booking a visit to Wembley

2nd: Chelsea (PL) A
9th: Shrewsbury Town (FA) H
13th: Arsenal (CC) H
16th: Brentford (PL) H
20th: Arsenal (CC) A
23rd: Crystal Palace (PL) A

Sunday, January 2nd, 4.30pm
Premier League
Chelsea 2, Liverpool 2

Goals: Mane (9), Salah (26)

Line-up: Kelleher, Alexander-Arnold, Konate, Van Dijk, Tsimikas, Henderson, Fabinho, Milner (Keita 69), Salah, Jota (Oxlade-Chamberlain 69), Mane (Jones 90). Subs not used: Gomez, Adrian, Beck, N Williams, Morton, Pitaluga

Pep Lijnders' post-match reaction: 'We should have controlled the game better. We had moments already before the 2-0; we were lethal in our counter-attacks. In the moments we played, we really connected well and we were quick in mind, thought about the next pass. The way we opened up spaces was incredible and we used these spaces really well in the whole game – maybe sometimes the last pass, maybe sometimes a better timing with our movement in behind to create even more. Overall, I can speak a lot about tactics and all these ideas but for me [the feeling is] pride because we could have come here with a lot of excuses, the team could have come here with a lot of excuses, but they fought with all they had. Getting a result away at Chelsea is always good, it is just we could have avoided it better if we'd played more football, more often better football in their half and they would not have had that many situations. We could have avoided these two goals with better defending. A title race is only decided on the last matchday and there are so many points to collect. We have this difficult situation and you never know if the opposition will get a difficult situation. We have to focus on ourselves, that's how we always did it, that's how we got into the position we are, that's how our team developed, how our team is in this moment in time. We only focus on the next game to make it a final and give everything we have and with this we become better. With this we became champions, we won the Champions League and we won the other two cups, so this is what we have to keep doing. Again, a big compliment to our team because if we keep this fighting spirit up and we play a little bit better, then we have a big chance as well in the next games.'

Post-match notes

Jürgen Klopp missed the game with a case of COVID. Pep Lijnders took on managerial duties for the match.

Jürgen Klopp

v Shrewsbury Town
Sunday, January 9th, 2pm

'THIS IS ONE OF THE STRANGEST PROGRAMME COLUMNS I HAVE EVER WRITTEN...'

FA Cup third round

January 2022

GOOD afternoon and welcome back to Anfield for our FA Cup match against Shrewsbury Town. I have to address this immediately: this is one of the strangest programme columns I have ever written, because I have no idea if I will be in the stadium with you, leading my team in person – or watching from home.

As you will know by now, I tested positive for COVID in the build-up to the Chelsea match and have been in isolation since, meaning I have been unable to have direct contact with my players or anyone else since.

At the time of writing this I have no idea if I will be in attendance at the game. That will depend on whether I am testing negative in line with the guidance.

What I can say is that I'm doing okay and looking forward to getting back to work. I thank God for the vaccination, because I did feel unwell during this but fortunately only mild illness really, and I'm certain that's because I've been privileged to have my jabs, including the booster.

Being disconnected from the team and staff was a strange experience. It hasn't happened often in my career and never for a length of time such as a full week.

Not that I needed it, but it did serve as a reminder of how blessed I am to have such wonderfully-talented staff supporting me and the boys. I didn't worry for one second that the quality of leadership for the players would be impacted.

Pep Lijnders, Pete Krawietz, Vitor Matos and all the other guys – from fitness coaches, to the medical and physio team, analysts and so on – did such a fantastic job in keeping our work environment to a level where the standards never drop.

I watched the game at Stamford Bridge from my living room and was so proud of our club.

Pep said it really well during his media duties before and after the game. We went there with so many challenges.

I was only one positive case – there were many others in and around that game, from players and staff. It makes such a big impact on your preparations.

This is not an excuse – it is a fact. You prepare a team for what is such an important game and then each day something changes which means you have to change. In our case this included right up until the day of the game itself.

This isn't unique to us and it's been with us now for much of December. But it does impact things far beyond inconvenience.

So, with all these issues, to have shown the courage and positivity we did at Chelsea made me feel pride.

Of course, the disruption around that match wasn't the end of our problems and I do want to address the postponement of the first leg of the League Cup tie against Arsenal.

It is not something we sought lightly and anyone who thinks otherwise clearly ignores how we have conducted ourselves as a club during this period. We have always looked to play, if feasible to do so.

For the game that would have been Thursday this week just gone, it was impossible. We asked for the game to be moved because we had no choice. It is the first time we have made such an appeal and we did so because we could not field a team.

On Tuesday the situation escalated from difficult to untenable. Another large number of positive test results were recorded within the group, added to the ones we already had, plus injuries and illness. We had to cancel training and eventually even shut the training ground itself.

We spoke to the local medical experts and this was their advice. Remember our group is fully vaccinated and still we had this.

So moving the game was the right decision and means from this weekend onwards we should now be in a position to put enough names on a team-sheet to fulfil fixtures again, because we have players returning from their isolation, including academy players who have been impacted.

I mentioned previously the gratitude I felt to my staff and that applies to the players just as much. Again, I emphasise what happens with us is not unique, far from it. Since December it's actually quite common across football, just as it has been in society. But for the boys it makes preparing for games far more challenging. Their attitude and application has remained at the highest level.

Today is a big test for us. I welcome Steve Cotterill, his players, staff, officials and supporters of Shrewsbury to Anfield for the game.

Earlier I talked about my own experiences with COVID and mercifully for me it was nothing too serious. I have read and listened to Mr Cotterill detailing what he went through after catching this illness and I am so pleased for him and his family he is over the worst of it now, back on his feet and back at work.

He spoke really well and movingly about how he suffered. If you haven't already I would encourage you to seek out a video or article where Steve details his battle back to health. It's inspiring actually.

As I say, I was moved by it, but educated also. It is a stark reminder why this awful thing is so serious and why we should all take measures to protect ourselves and each other while this pandemic is still with us.

We haven't faced each other as managers before, I don't think, but I know Steve is a highly experienced football leader and a fierce competitor. From the analysis we have done it is clear his teams reflect his own personality: brilliantly-organised and drilled, a clear plan, fighters – and belief in themselves and what they do. They are a very good team.

Steve and his players will relish this opportunity. I have no doubt they come here today believing and probably expecting to defeat us. They want that place in round four just as much as us. We have to respect their quality and understand how dangerous they are as an opponent.

What is clear is we must work harder than they will or we will not get the result we desire. That is the most important task. Our level of commitment must surpass theirs. If we do that, I am hopeful we will have a positive afternoon.

Finally – and it's a return to my feeling of pride in how the club has conducted itself in recent weeks – while we have faced these many challenges, our supporters are, as always, an integral part of that.

How they have backed the team during this period has been something else. The problem when detailing the issues we contend with, as a football team, is that you know even as you say it that in comparison to wider society these are problems of the privileged.

Be it issues around preparing a team or the impact of the schedule, we all know these problems don't stack up in significance when compared to those faced by the people who make great sacrifices to support us. We talk about football issues because we are a football team, so they are ours and impact us. It is information that is relevant to us.

I am not a silly person, therefore along with my team I know the hardships our fans contend with are far more real. So to see them come to Anfield or travel to away games and give the level of passion and commitment to helping us through matches is humbling. It really is.

I could hear it through the TV when watching the Chelsea game. They gave all their energy to our players. We appreciate it like crazy.

Hopefully today we can give you a performance and result that proves we never take it for granted.

Liverpool 4, Shrewsbury Town 1

Goals: Gordon (34), Fabinho (44pen, 90+3), Firmino (78)

Line-up: Kelleher, Bradley, Konate, Van Dijk, Robertson (Tsimikas 90+2), Dixon-Bonner (Firmino 64), Fabinho, Morton (Norris 90+2), Gordon (Frauendorf 81), Woltman (Minamino 46), Jones. Subs not used: Adrian, Matip, Mabaya, Balagizi

Jürgen's post-match reaction: 'This was the team we could line up today and the boys did really well in a difficult game, which became even more difficult when we conceded for 1-0. But the boys reacted well, put in a really proper shift, and it's so difficult because setting up a team, starting training again on Friday and then involving all these young kids. They are all really good footballers, there's no doubt about that, we are not in doubt about that, so that's all good. But it makes it really tricky, especially when you have to play and break down a low block, which Shrewsbury, rightly so, did today. So, I am just happy about the result, happy that we went through and about a lot of things – that Taki trained only twice now after his injury, actually rather still part of the rehab the game today than a real game. Then Bobby came back only yesterday for training and played now in the game and scored as well. So many things could have gone the wrong way today and in the end we made it all fine.'

Post-match notes

Liverpool's team contained four teenagers – Kaide Gordon, Conor Bradley, Elijah Dixon-Bonner and Max Woltman. Gordon netted his first Liverpool goal in the game. This was the first game Liverpool were without AFCON participants Mo Salah, Sadio Mane and Naby Keita.

v Arsenal
Thursday, January 13th, 7.45pm

'WE DESPERATELY WANT TO WIN THIS TROPHY – BUT SO DO THREE OTHER TEAMS'

Carabao Cup semi-final, first leg

GOOD evening and welcome back to Anfield for our Carabao Cup semi-final match against Arsenal. I welcome Mikel Arteta, his players, staff, officials and the supporters of Arsenal for their visit.

It is not the first time that we have played each other in our home this season, and therefore I have spoken at length previously about Mikel and his team in these pages.

Nothing has changed in that regard. My respect for him as a leader of his club could not be higher. What he does in this moment is clear. They improve week-on-week. They are a proper force again. Upwardly mobile as a team, for sure. Full of energy. Full of belief and confidence.

Mikel and his staff know exactly how he wants them to play. They are a threat for any team.

A game like this is different because it is the first of a two-legged tie. I know there is a match to win for both of us and it's still just 90 minutes. But knowing when the whistle goes tonight at full-time, we are effectively half-time overall, is different.

Both clubs have massive experience of two-legged football because of our respective European adventures, so I think it's fair to say the players will know tonight is about playing each and every second of the contest with all they have.

Every second counts this evening. What you do with

the last kick of this game could be as important as the first.

This will be our attitude for sure. We desperately want to win this trophy. But so do three other teams, including Arsenal.

I did address this in the programme column last weekend, so don't want to overly repeat myself, but it would be odd not to comment that tonight is the first leg and not the second because of the postponement.

Not being able to play seven days ago was absolutely the last thing any of us would have wished to happen. If you don't believe that then sorry, I can't help you with explanation. Our situation was so extreme that eventually the decision was made to close our training facilities.

At that point not only could we not field a team, we also could not prepare one.

COVID is still very much with us, as Mikel and I have experienced first-hand recently. It's a situation that makes preparing a team extremely difficult. But extremely difficulty is okay – when something becomes impossible, it is not okay.

I think the eventual solution makes sense. It was the only decision really. It is right we are at Anfield tonight and it is the first leg here now. It would have been extremely unfair on supporters to have any more disruption because of issues beyond all our control.

Getting a team on the pitch for the weekend against Shrewsbury Town was a challenge but we did so with minimal preparation time. I myself only joined up with the squad on the Sunday morning but that was the least of our issues.

Players who were coming back from injury, such as Taki, got to train on Friday and Saturday only and then used the minutes in the FA Cup almost as additional rehab. Other players were not long back from a COVID absence. I said afterwards that it was the only team we could pick and that wasn't meant in any way to downplay its quality, it was just a fact.

All that considered, I was very pleased with how they applied themselves. It was an assured and mature performance from our experienced players. They knew how strange and disrupted the preparation was. Most of them had to rely on instinct to navigate their way through.

For our younger players, it really was a fantastic effort and I'm very grateful for how they performed for this team and the club.

I am never short of a positive word to say about the work our academy guys do. They help to nurture players who are exceptional young men as well as very talented athletes. Their hunger to learn is what stands out.

They come to us with a freshness and eagerness to absorb all the knowledge and experience of the more established stars around them. That is because of the outstanding LFC Academy staff. The environment they create, the culture.

Ultimately the young players must be receptive, and how they adapt and integrate is very much down to them. If you ask any of our first team they will tell you we are blessed with an exceptional group.

There were a lot of 'firsts' on Sunday against Shrewsbury and it has been a season of 'firsts' for many of these younger pros. The crucial thing for them now is to make sure the 'firsts' turn into 'first of many' and definitely not into 'lasts'.

The opportunity at this club is always there. I've referenced the outstanding football education they get in the Academy but within my first-team staff they also have amazing champions.

Pep, Pete and Vitor invest themselves wholeheartedly into developing these talents so they can be ready to play in the senior set-up. Likewise John, Jack and Taffarel with the young keepers.

The effort on Sunday wasn't just limited to the pitch. I thought the ground made a big difference in showing patience during a contest where it was needed.

Tonight will be different I'm sure for many reasons. It's a semi-final. It's under the lights. And it's an opponent with whom we have a really strong rivalry. It has always felt like a rivalry built on mutual respect, I must say.

I've written before that this fixture always has a sparkle around it, both in the build-up and on the night.

I think Arsenal under Mikel are about as exciting and adventurous an opponent as you could face. It makes it a really cool challenge. And it's an opportunity. Opportunity for players and supporters.

A place in the final is what we will fight for, albeit over two games. We can and will give all we have, starting this evening at Anfield.

As always, I hope we can perform to a level that makes our fans proud.

Liverpool 0, Arsenal 0

Line-up: Alisson, Alexander-Arnold (N Williams 75), Matip (Gomez 76), Van Dijk, Robertson, Henderson, Fabinho (Oxlade-Chamberlain 75), Milner (Jones 61), Jota, Firmino, Minamino. Subs not used: Konate, Tsimikas, Gordon, Kelleher, Morton

Jürgen's post-match reaction: 'First and foremost, I don't think even you saw this for the first time in the history of football – things like this happen. Our situation – and I said it before and it's not an excuse, it's an explanation – [meant] for obvious reasons we had to change the line-up tonight. I really liked the way we started in the game, I saw absolutely everything we wanted to see in the beginning. Front-footed, lively, direct in the right moments, we switched it in the right moments. We started in the game like we wanted to start and then there was the red card and then we play against a low block. Against a low block with the most finely-tuned team is difficult and obviously we are not – then on top of that, we made a few wrong decisions, we felt too much rushed, it looked like all of sudden we felt under pressure, which doesn't make sense but it looked for me a little bit like that. It is a typical situation. This is a cup competition, it is a two-leg semi-final, it is half-time, it is 0-0 and even when probably Arsenal feels in a better position at the moment we don't feel this tie is over for us so we will give it another proper try next Thursday.'

Post-match notes

Arsenal's Granit Xhaka was sent off in the first half but Liverpool couldn't find the breakthrough to take an advantage into the second leg.

January 2022

v Brentford
Sunday, January 16th, 2pm

'ANFIELD IS THE BEST ENERGY SOURCE IN WORLD SPORT. WE WILL BE PLUGGED IN AT TIMES TODAY'

Premier League

GOOD afternoon and welcome back to Anfield for our Premier League match against Brentford. I welcome Thomas Frank, his players, staff, officials and the supporters of our visitors.

What a story Brentford's is. I love what they do. Because of where they have come from, in terms of progression through the leagues, it is often described as a fairy tale, but I don't think that is a fair description at all. It fails to recognise their success is built on having a clear plan, sticking to the plan and having outstandingly talented people to carry it out.

I am such a big fan of Thomas. What a guy! And what a football leader. He is clearly 100 per cent in his work. He is knowledgeable and passionate. Albeit judging from the outside, I think there is a synergy between him, his players and the supporters which he has clearly played the biggest part in creating.

It's our second meeting with Brentford, having already played the game against them at their home in London and we are expecting just as difficult a contest today as we experienced down there. They are brave. They are full of energy. They will be on the front-foot for sure. That's cool. It makes for a great football match.

I am writing this column prior to the League Cup game against Arsenal midweek, so cannot make any reference to our performance or result there.

We are in the period now whereby we have these

matches with three players currently away at the Africa Cup of Nations.

Firstly, for the three guys – Sadio, Naby and Mo – I wish them nothing but joy, luck and success while competing in this great competition.

At the time of writing this, all three have played their opening group games, with varying experiences. Sadio and Naby got off to a winning start, but unfortunately for Mo his afternoon was a little more frustrating.

We are all following the matches on TV and, as a team, we are supporting all three when their respective nations are in action. By the time these words are public the game will have already taken place, but Senegal v Guinea was always going to be a little more complicated emotionally. Hopefully it finished 3-3 with both our boys grabbing hat-tricks!

Hand on heart I would love one of them to go all the way and become champions. I know what it means to them. I hope they enjoy every second of their time competing.

For us, it means we must play without them, including today, until they return. But that is absolutely fine.

It presents fantastic opportunity for other players. This is how we view it.

It's a topic I have often spoken about, but it is so true that to be successful the entire squad has a role to play. We never view it as first choices in terms of team selection actually. It's about the right team for the specific fixture.

This is an intense period and each and every player's contribution will be critical, if we are to get the results we want.

Every second of every game is opportunity for us if we are minded to view it as such. We can't switch off even for the briefest of moments and we must not lose focus. We have to be in every moment. We must be ready in every moment.

The quality of the opponent is too strong for us to be anything other than our best at all times.

These comments apply to Anfield as well, although I know that like my players, the fans need no reminding. I get it that early afternoon kick-offs in January are not always the most famous times for producing magic, but they can be if we are minded so. This has been our collective story over the past years. We write our own story, together.

The impact from the supporters will be as crucial today as a European night. It's actually one of my favourite things about our club: how knowledgeable and perceptive our supporters are. They can sense when we need them.

Today will absolutely be one of those days. When Anfield is on its toes it doesn't matter what time of day it is, or whether floodlights are needed. It is the best energy source in world sport and we will be plugged in at times today for sure.

Finally, to conclude these notes, I am aware of the campaign for a Hillsborough Law which has recently been proposed.

I want to have a better understanding of why this is so important and is actually far bigger than just a Liverpool issue or even a football issue.

There is actually no bigger concern for any country than the families of victims and survivors of tragedies being protected from further injustice.

As I have said many times previously, the best people to listen to when you want to better inform yourself and learn about something is a person with knowledge.

Our captain, Jordan Henderson, has given his matchday programme column to Sir Kenny Dalglish today, so this subject can be spoken about by someone with detailed expertise of what this campaign means and why it is so important that we all support it where we can.

If, like me, you want and need a better understanding of this, I hope you read Sir Kenny's words today.

They will be the most important ones written in this publication.

Liverpool 3, Brentford 0

Goals: Fabinho (44), Oxlade-Chamberlain (69), Minamino (77)

Line-up: Alisson, Alexander-Arnold, Matip, Van Dijk, Robertson, Henderson, Fabinho, Jones, Oxlade-Chamberlain (Minamino 74), Firmino (Milner 78), Jota (Gordon 82). Subs not used: Konate, Gomez, Tsimikas, Kelleher, N Williams, Morton

Jürgen's post-match reaction: 'The way Brentford plays against us is really uncomfortable. As the team at home, if you want to and have to win the game then you want to control the game. To control this game is particularly difficult because the ball felt like it was 20 minutes in the air today and there were so many situations – header, header, header, header, header. So you need to be full of desire in these moments to sort it. You have to bring the ball down on the floor and from there you have to play, so it's really tricky and that's why I'm so happy. The game against Brentford – I knew before that it would be a really tough one – it was a tough one and that's why I'm so happy that we did so well in other moments. We showed the boys at half-time three situations where we did really well in the first half. [We] scored on top of that a goal from a set-piece, which is absolutely helpful. I think apart from a spell in the second half when they took a bit more risk, we needed a little bit too long to adapt to it, but in the moment when we adapted we controlled the game again, scored really nice goals and I'm really happy about it.'

Post-match notes

This was the first time since May 2017 that Liverpool had lined up for a Premier League game without both Sadio Mane and Mo Salah. Kaide Gordon made his Premier League debut.

Thursday, January 20th, 7.45pm
Carabao Cup semi-final, second leg
Arsenal 0, Liverpool 2
(Liverpool win 2-0 on aggregate)

Goals: Jota (19, 77)

Line-up: Kelleher, Alexander-Arnold, Matip (Konate 46), Van Dijk, Robertson, Henderson (Milner 75), Fabinho, Jones, Gordon (Minamino 63), Firmino (N Williams 84), Jota. Subs not used: Alisson, Gomez, Adrian, Tsimikas, Morton

Jürgen's post-match reaction: 'The mood in the dressing room is over the moon. Difficult game, difficult time but the boys were exceptional. First half, Arsenal started lively, then we calmed it down, played good football and created plenty. Second half similar. We scored two wonderful goals, Diogo Jota on fire. We were completely convinced when he arrived at the club he would help us massively. Since he is here he has turned into a really world-class striker. Mentality mixed with quality is the reason we signed him. He is incredibly important to us. He is in good shape as well and long may it continue.'

Post-match notes

This 2-0 aggregate win secured a record 13th League Cup final for the Reds. It would be the Reds' first Wembley final for six years. Arsenal had Thomas Partey sent off in the closing minutes.

Sunday, January 23rd, 2pm
Premier League
Crystal Palace 1 Liverpool 3

Goals: Van Dijk (8), Oxlade-Chamberlain (32), Fabinho (89pen)

Line-up: Alisson, Alexander-Arnold (Gomez 90+2), Matip, Van Dijk, Robertson, Henderson, Fabinho, Jones, Oxlade-Chamberlain (Minamino 60), Firmino (Milner 90), Jota. Subs not used: Konate, Tsimikas, Gordon, Kelleher, N Williams, Morton

Jürgen's post-match reaction: 'It was a bit Jekyll and Hyde football today, to be honest. We saw how good we can be – we were incredibly good in the first 35 minutes, I would say. Then, after an intense week, we had an away game at Arsenal that was really intense as well, and then flying back, coming here, so I don't have a real explanation, to be honest, but intensity might be an explanation. And we became sloppy in the last line. The chances we gave them in the first half were pretty much produced by us, the wrong pass, bah, bah, bah. Then, second half, we were not compact, the first line pressed too high. The distance was not right, so they just played the long balls in behind; I don't know why they were never offside, our fault of course. So, all of a sudden the game opened up and then you have to fight back, that's what the boys did. We were brilliant for 35 minutes and the opposite in the rest of the game. A massive relief. I didn't see it back but I don't think I have to because VAR thought it's a penalty, the ref saw it as a penalty. That the Crystal Palace people thought it's no penalty, I understand. But I think that's the proof you need. And then, well taken by Fab. A big three points today for us, really big. Intense period again. Now a little bit of a breather, which helps, at least for most of us, not for all of us – the Brazilians have to go, Taki has to go. But the rest can take a deep breath and then we start again.'

Post-match notes

A big win at Selhurst Park meant the Reds achieved maximum points in the Premier League while Mo Salah, Sadio Mane and Naby Keita were at the Africa Cup of Nations.

FEB

2022

Seven games brought seven victories as the Reds went goal crazy against Leeds, produced a glorious away performance in the Champions League at one of the great cathedrals of European football – and finished the month off at another superb venue where they collected the League Cup for the ninth time in the club's history

6th: Cardiff City (FA) H
10th: Leicester City (PL) H
13th: Burnley (PL) A
16th: Internazionale (CL) A
19th: Norwich City (PL) H
23rd: Leeds United (PL) H
27th: Chelsea (CC) N

v Cardiff City
Sunday, February 6th, 12pm

'LUIS HAS POTENTIAL FOR THE FUTURE BUT THE ABILITY TO HELP NOW ALSO'

FA Cup fourth round

Jürgen Klopp

GOOD afternoon and welcome back to Anfield for our FA Cup match against Cardiff City.

I welcome Steve Morison, his staff, players, officials and supporters of our visitors.

I know Steve is relatively new in his job leading the first team, having taken over earlier in the season, but it is clear from the analysis we have done he is already putting his stamp on the team and club. He took over with them having a difficult time in the Championship, but I think they have all the tools and leadership to steer away from danger and enjoy a more stable second half of the season.

Steve was an internal appointment, I believe, having started his coaching career with younger age groups when he retired from playing. This is such a smart pathway and I wish him and his staff nothing but success for the rest of the season – after today, of course.

Today will be really tough for us. We know Cardiff will see this as a massive opportunity for themselves. We know they will come with an expectation of winning. We know they will be on the front foot. So we have to be ready. It really is that simple.

Both of us come into the game in very different circumstances. As a club and team we have had a brief 'break' from matches, with no fixture last weekend. Cardiff, in contrast, have been playing pretty constantly and in games of real significance for them.

So they have rhythm and we have a degree of freshness.

It is, of course, important to remember the break was only for some of us. Our African players have been doing themselves and their nations proud in AFCON. Many of our South American players, plus Taki Minamino for Japan, have been involved in important games with extensive travelling. So we come into this game with a variety of challenges in terms of player availability.

At the time of writing this column both Sadio and Mo are through to the semi-finals, but Naby has returned home having enjoyed a fantastic tournament for him personally despite a slightly earlier exit. Whatever happens in the respective semi-finals we won't have Sadio or Mo home this weekend because there is the 3rd/4th place decider. By the time this column is public, the outcome will be known, but if it is a Senegal vs Egypt final all we can say back here is 'may the best team win'. We love and cherish them both. It's gutting they can't both come home with winner's medals.

I want to use these pages also to formally welcome Luis Diaz to the LFC family. At the time of this going to print he hasn't arrived with us as a group at AXA yet, but that is pending. I have no idea while writing this whether he can or will be involved today.

But regardless, I know it's a signing that has caused excitement with our fans and that's really cool. It's good to be excited and optimistic about something. I love the energy that comes with that.

It's a smart piece of business for the club, I must say, and it was very well-managed and secured by our football ops team, with the support of ownership and Mike Gordon in particular.

I don't want to go into chapter and verse about Luis' qualities, because soon enough he'll have the chance to display them himself. What he does will be far more important than anything I say. But in terms of helping the team, the squad and club, it's fantastic we made this happen.

I'm sure supporters are usually sick of my answers to transfer questions in press conferences, because we don't give much away. But what is clear is this is a player who we think has potential for the future but the ability to help now also. I've been very clear in the past: the only players you should look to sign in the January window are players who you'd want in the summer. That is very much the case with Luis.

We also saw a couple of players leave, albeit on loan. Nat Phillips and Neco Williams will be battling for promotion from the Championship between now and May. Magnificent opportunity for both. And both Bournemouth and Fulham are very fortunate to get these two outstanding young men.

Their Liverpool stories are not over – they are merely

on pause – so I don't want my words to feel like a farewell. But both these players have made a massive contribution to our club in recent seasons. The way they were day-to-day made us better collectively. When they played they produced the goods. I couldn't be more grateful towards them both and I hope they show all their talent and quality in the coming days, weeks and months.

When I looked at the Championship table I noticed they are pretty close together at the top. I hope we don't have another situation like the potential final meeting between Senegal and Egypt, where it's only one of them who can be truly satisfied in the end. Fingers crossed both Nat and Neco will be celebrating promotion come May. They are two boys who deserve success.

Finally, I am conscious we kick off at 12 midday today. To be clear and leave no doubt: this will not be a factor for the result. But it is a factor for preparation and atmosphere.

I have yet to meet anyone who plays football who punches the air when a kick-off is really early as opposed to later in the day such as afternoon or evening. I have to admit I haven't met many supporters who celebrate a kick-off at lunchtime either. And yes, I know this is something clubs are just as responsible for also. Clubs are part-and-parcel of the decision-making. It's not my intention to open the box on that discussion in this column. Clubs share responsibility for this, but it's players and fans who feel the impact.

However, a kick-off time such as this makes the response of the crowd even more important. We haven't played a match in two weeks and therefore I think the energy from the supporters will be more valuable anyway.

It's always on us to bring the performance regardless and I have always been clear the responsibility to make Anfield alive falls to us in the first instance. Given how important this game is and how motivated Cardiff City will be to beat us, I think the intensity on the pitch will be at the highest levels.

I'm informed there is a big following coming from Wales for our visitors and I remember from playing Cardiff previously their fans are full of passion and voice. That's cool – really cool. It means Anfield needs to be on its toes also.

Midday or not, it's a day of opportunity and we are together again, in our home with a match that needs to be won. Let's give it all we have.

Liverpool 3, Cardiff City 1

Goals: Jota (53), Minamino (68), Elliott (76)

Line-up: Kelleher, Alexander-Arnold, Konate, Van Dijk, Tsimikas (Robertson 70), Henderson (Thiago 78), Keita (Elliott 58), Jones (Diaz 58), Minamino (Milner 69), Firmino, Jota. Subs not used: Adrian, Matip, Gordon, Morton

Jürgen's post-match reaction: 'With the goal [from Harvey Elliott] it became obviously a proper fairy tale to be honest. In my mind I had the situation, it's not nice but it came up, in Leeds when we lost him with this horrible injury. All the way through he was very patient and our medical department did obviously an incredible job with him, but he was patient enough to do all the necessary steps. Coming on is already a great step back, but scoring this nice goal makes it a proper fairy tale so I am really happy for him. He was over the moon! It was properly touching. So, all good. When Luis [Diaz] went down it was a scary moment, that's true. The goal he set up for Taki was absolutely incredible: high press, counter-press, I love it, and then Taki finished it off. Then, the long ball, the heading challenge, he goes down [and] holds his knee afterwards. We were all really shocked. I had a look on the screen and I saw that everything was fine in the air, everything was fine when he came down, but then I saw the big fella of Cardiff standing on his knee and he has now a bruise there and a scar, it's red and a little bit open. We all said to him, 'Welcome to England!' Now he has his first assist and his first little scar. That's absolutely okay.'

Post-match notes

Luis Diaz made his Reds debut after completing his move from Porto. Harvey Elliott made his first appearance after suffering a dreadful ankle injury in September, and scored Liverpool's second goal.

v Leicester City
Thursday, February 10th, 7.45pm

'I FEEL BLESSED EVERY DAY TO HAVE THE OPPORTUNITY TO WORK WITH MO AND SADIO'

Premier League

GOOD evening and welcome back to Anfield for our Premier League fixture against Leicester City. I welcome back, for the second time in the space of a couple of months, Brendan Rodgers, his staff, players officials and supporters of the visitors.

Given we played here, albeit in the Carabao Cup, not too long ago I don't really need to go into my thoughts, feelings and admiration for Brendan again in great detail. We also played a league fixture at their place a matter of weeks ago, which is more relevant in terms of what to expect.

Leicester were outstanding that night and as I said after the game itself, we could have no complaints about the outcome. It serves as a reminder of the qualities Brendan, his team and his club have when faced with adversity and we have to be mindful of that tonight.

I know they had a tough afternoon on Sunday in the FA Cup, but if anything our recent experience teaches us that will make them more dangerous as an opponent.

For the game in Leicester – just after Christmas – Brendan and his coaches faced challenges which I would consider almost overwhelming. But they demonstrated their quality and character that night and we suffered as a result. We have to be mindful of this and we must be ready. Ready for an opposition that is hungry, focused, brilliantly-organised, with a clear plan.

Tonight will be as tough as any game we could

play, against any opponent. The cool thing is we have those same qualities in our group. We have desire, we have belief in ourselves and we see the game as an opportunity. We have outstanding players. It feels like a big-match night and an important one, and that's really cool. It's the most important game of our season because it's the next one. That's how we focus coming into it. And we give it our all.

The weekend for us was satisfying for a number of reasons. The result of course, but also a number of side stories around it.

I'm conscious of overplaying the situation with Harvey Elliott, because it's critically important now we all realise he will still need time and patience to fully reintegrate and get to the consistent levels we expect of him and he expects of himself. But you'd need a heart of stone not to be moved by what happened. What a moment.

It was apparent after the game, when our players were showing their love and joy towards Harvey, that there was a recurring theme: hard work pays off. And what I loved about Harvey's own comments post-match is that he was the first to recognise the hard work wasn't only his. His comeback actually started seconds after he suffered the injury and continued right up until the moment he ran back onto the Anfield pitch on Sunday in the 58th minute.

Chris Morgan (physio) and Jim Moxon (doctor) made critically important decisions on the pitch at Elland Road that day which protected Harvey when he was at his most vulnerable. They had a split-second to make those calls and they made all the right ones. The surgeon and doctors who cared for him in hospital likewise.

Then when the focus turned to recovery it was Joe Lewis who picked up the baton, with a plan mapped out and overseen by Andreas Schlumberger. Harvey name-checked Joe in his post-match interview and there is a reason for that. The care and treatment he got was best-in-class. And not just physical care but emotional and mental support also.

When it came time to be back on grass, Dave Rydings was a pivotal figure, again working with Andreas Schlumberger and Joe. My office at the AXA Training Centre overlooks the pitches and I lost count of the days I would watch those sessions and see the player get stronger with every sprint, jump and kick.

I highlight all of this not because I think what's happened with Harvey is in any way a miracle or even that extraordinary. The opposite actually. It's what we expected. A top professional, even if very young, with an elite attitude to his work. Allied with knowledgeable and dedicated staff, eager to use their expertise to help make the process the best it could possibly be.

I want to highlight it because it's important to

acknowledge the collective effort that goes into making a team successful. I've missed out dozens of other people who play a role in moments such as helping a player through an injury and rehab, including all the staff, from coaches to admin guys, in and around our training ground.

There is the famous proverb: 'It takes a village to raise a child'. And that applies also in a healthy football environment and we certainly have it at LFC. It is a community of people which makes this team what it is. The whole is greater than the sum of our parts and it's nice to have relevant examples to remind ourselves of that.

The other topic I want to address, although I won't exhaust the detail, is the AFCON final and the return of two heroes.

I could not be prouder of Mo and Sadio. Legends and leaders forever now, not that we at Liverpool needed any extra evidence. Of course congratulations to Sadio for becoming a champion.

I know as well as anyone how much he has craved winning this trophy for Senegal. Player of the tournament as well was richly deserved. I could not be more pleased for him. But love and admiration for both in terms of the contributions they made to their country during this period.

Mo and Sadio are world-class men as well as

world-class athletes. Ambassadors and role-models for society as a whole, well beyond the borders of their own nations or the LFC family.

I feel blessed every day to have the opportunity to work with them. What is really cool is just how hungry they remain for even more success. It's great to have them back with us.

I'm not sure whether they'll be involved in the match tonight, but the next time they are with us I know our supporters will express their own congratulations.

Hopefully this evening we can show again how much representing LFC means to all of us: players, management and fans. I hope we put in a performance to make the supporters proud.

Liverpool 2, Leicester City 0

Goals: Jota (34, 87)

Line-up: Alisson, Alexander-Arnold, Matip, Van Dijk, Robertson, Thiago, Fabinho, Jones (Elliott 60), Jota, Firmino (Salah 60), Diaz (Minamino 90). Subs not used: Konate, Milner, Keita, Oxlade-Chamberlain, Tsimikas, Kelleher

Jürgen's post-match reaction: 'I saw a lot of good football tonight but there were moments when I wished we would have controlled the game a little bit more, when we gave Leicester at least a bit too much possession. It didn't lead to anything properly, that they had massive chances or things like that, but it costs you energy and we could have invested that in the other direction. But anyhow, it was two wonderful goals, could have scored more and we are the deserved winner. So, I'm really happy about that. First and foremost we have to win our football games. This football club is massive and since I'm here I can't remember a game we lost and everybody said, 'Yeah, you can lose that game.' It's always the same situation: there's a game, we put on the shirts and then we have to win it. It doesn't work out all the time but thank God, it happened a couple of times. That's the situation we are in. It was really important for us tonight to win, because there's not only Man City to catch or whatever, there are a lot of teams in behind us who want to get closer – and that's a very important task as well.'

Post-match notes

Luis Diaz made his first start for the club while Mo Salah made his first appearance since his return from the Africa Cup of Nations.

Sunday, February 13th, 2pm
Premier League
Burnley 0, Liverpool 1

Goal: Fabinho (40)

Line-up: Alisson, Alexander-Arnold, Matip, Van Dijk, Robertson, Henderson (Thiago 59), Fabinho, Keita (Milner 90+2), Salah, Firmino, Mane (Jota 67). Subs not used: Konate, Oxlade-Chamberlain, Tsimikas, Diaz, Kelleher, Elliott

Jürgen's post-match reaction: 'I am absolutely delighted with the way we played the circumstances, it was so tricky. Only if you stood on the pitch I think you could really feel the wind to the whole extent. But the boys deal with it. Obviously over the years my teams learned to deal with the circumstances and that is not speaking too much about it before the game. We ask ourselves to use it instead of suffering from it, that's what happens when you are longer here. So, really, a difficult game. I am really happy. Today, complete adults' football was needed and that's what the boys delivered. I am really happy about that.'

Post-match notes

Fabinho's winner made it five goals in seven games for the midfielder. Sadio Mane made his first appearance since returning from the Africa Cup of Nations.

Wednesday, February 16th, 8pm
Champions League round of 16, first leg
Internazionale 0, Liverpool 2

Goals: Firmino (75), Salah (83)

Line-up: Alisson, Alexander-Arnold, Konate, Van Dijk, Robertson, Elliott (Keita 59), Fabinho (Henderson 60), Thiago (Milner 86), Salah, Jota (Firmino 46), Mane (Diaz 59). Subs not used: Gomez, Oxlade-Chamberlain, Minamino, Tsimikas, Origi, Matip, Kelleher

Jürgen's post-match reaction: 'It is still dangerous. It is half-time and nothing else. That's how it is in the knockout stages, you learn a lot about an opponent. If it is a proper half-time like today and we are 2-0 up at half-time, I don't tell the boys, 'Job done, put your legs on the table', it is a very tricky result so why should we think differently about it now? I thought defensively it was a really strong performance, but it would be silly if we wouldn't defend well because it means a lot to us this competition and these games, so we invested a lot and it's good.'

Post-match notes

Liverpool secured their second San Siro win of the season as Harvey Elliott became the youngest player to start a Champions League game for the Reds, aged 18 years and 318 days.

February 2022

v Norwich City
Saturday, February 19th, 3pm

'FOR EVERY ASSIST AND GOAL, THERE IS A CONTRIBUTION ELSEWHERE THAT IS JUST AS IMPORTANT'

Premier League

Jürgen Klopp

GOOD afternoon and welcome to Anfield for our Premier League fixture against Norwich City. I welcome Dean Smith, his players, staff, officials and the supporters of our visitors.

First and foremost, I was a big fan of Daniel Farke and was personally disappointed to see him leave the Premier League. Cool guy and a very good manager.

However, on the flip-side it was fantastic to see Dean back so soon after his departure from Aston Villa. What a job Dean and his staff did there. It's easy to forget where Villa were when he took over. Their current status in the Premier League was a world away from realistic expectation.

Dean must be so proud of all he achieved there, particularly as it was his hometown club and one that meant so much to his family.

Norwich, I'm sure, consider themselves fortunate to have a man like him leading them now. Already he has made his influence known. We will have to face Dean's Norwich here twice in relatively quick succession because of the FA Cup draw. Two really hard games against a highly-motivated opponent.

We know we face a well-organised set of players, with a lot of quality and fighting for their lives, with a manager who knows how to keep a club in this league, even when circumstances are tough. We are in for a real fight today.

February 2022

Because of print deadlines I am writing this ahead of our game against Inter Milan. Whatever the outcome, the tie will only be at half-time, so it doesn't really matter what I say on this. Either way, there will be a job to finish. Of course the fact that we played in midweek and Norwich did not is a factor today, but I don't see it as an advantage or disadvantage in either direction. We have rhythm and they have rest. It's just information.

Because we are still involved in all cup competitions, including Europe, it's something we are used to.

There are challenges for the players and also us as coaches. We have to make the right calls in terms of how we deploy our resources. The players need to make sure they are right mentally and physically.

The first part of that is crucial. Tiredness, as an athlete, can live in the mind just as much as the legs. We need to ensure we free our minds of it. Focus on the opportunity the next game presents.

We have the best environment imaginable to recover, prepare and go again. Make the most of it. View the situation purely as information. Use previous experiences and attack the matchday.

As a group of players they do this incredibly well. As a group they relish matchday. So that's great for us as coaches. Our responsibility to the team is to make the right decisions for the benefit of the collective as often as possible. That's management.

Although I can't offer any insight into our trip to Italy in this column, I can look back to our last Premier League fixture, away to Burnley.

It was a brilliant display of character and game-management from the players. There were some big individual contributions as always, but it was the collective effort which meant we left one of the most difficult away trips with all three points.

I do want to make a mention of our number four, our centre-half. The level Virgil has performed to this season has been incredible. When you factor in what he's returning from it's even more remarkable.

It was always clear, because the surgery was a complete success, that Virg would be absolutely fine medium and long-term. But the truth is given everything that happened, the level he is at so quickly is a surprise, to be honest. Well, I'll correct that: it would be a surprise were it not Virgil.

I'd have to check but I think it's been 16 clean sheets this season so far for games he's been on the pitch for. Not conceding in a game isn't the only marker for a defender's form, but it is important.

I only bring this up because I think there is sometimes a danger that certain players can be taken for granted. Externally I mean – never internally – we would never allow this.

Often this is due to the expectation they've set

themselves from previous performance levels or maybe a failure to appreciate that the role they're performing benefits the team over themselves.

As a manager and coaching staff we never judge a player's value on moments that go viral via social media clips. For every assist and goal there is a contribution and sacrifice elsewhere on the pitch that's just as important. To have a successful team you must first have a balanced team.

What distinguishes Liverpool supporters, in my view, is they have that knowledge and education to appreciate the players who sacrifice just as much as those who generate headlines. It's so important in a successful team environment.

Finally, I was told earlier this week that Liverpool FC has received three nominations in the British LGBT Awards. Wow! As well as being humbled and honoured that we are thought about this way, I am also proud because these kinds of nominations show who we are and the values that we represent.

As a manager I will always be judged by the number of games we win and how successful we are and this is the way it should be. But the importance of being part of an organisation that stands up for equality, inclusivity and tolerance is so vital that it is hard to put into words.

These are values that I strongly believe everyone should cherish, but I know that this is not always the case so I count myself fortunate to be at a club and to live in a city where they are not just accepted, they are championed.

I don't know whether we will be lucky enough to win, especially seeing as the other nominees in the three categories are so incredible and so impressive, but this is definitely a situation in which we should take a lot of pride from just making the shortlist.

But whatever the outcome, we should use it as an inspiration to be even better still. Our friends and allies in the LGBT community deserve nothing less.

I hope our supporters enjoy the match today and are in no doubt of the important role they have to play.

This is the sort of game where they are critical. Make Anfield full of intensity. Be there in moments the team needs it. The LFC crowd know their role. They know their importance.

Liverpool 3, Norwich City 1

Goals: Mane (64), Salah (67), Diaz (81)

Line-up: Alisson, Gomez, Matip, Van Dijk, Tsimikas, Oxlade-Chamberlain (Thiago 62), Henderson, Keita (Origi 62), Salah, Mane, Diaz (Minamino 90).
Subs not used: Fabinho, Konate, Milner, Robertson, Kelleher, Elliott

Jürgen's post-match reaction: 'We could have scored really early in the game with two massive chances from Kostas and the other one was the header from Virgil when he squared the ball and I thought there were two players from us who could have finished it off. Then, you don't score, they find a little better in the game. It is a really good football team. Dean is obviously doing an incredible job – very talented, very brave, very confident. But half-time, it was not that we said we had to change this, this and this. Actually, we showed one longer sequence where we played exactly like we should have played all the time. We just should have done it more often. We tried that in the second half obviously but then we concede that goal and you could see directly a few minutes after, it was now a bit hectic, the atmosphere was hectic, everyone got a bit nervous. We thought it made sense to make that early change just to calm it directly down again. We did that literally obviously, with Thiago and a system change to 4-4-2. Then anyway you have to finish the situations off. The first goal was not the biggest chance we had in the game, Sadio just scored off it with an incredible finish. And the other goals were really beautiful as well. Yes, it was complicated, no problem with that. It's Premier League, you can see what kind of quality all the teams have. But that makes it so special when you win them then anyway.'

Post-match notes

Mo Salah scored his 150th goal for Liverpool in all competitions in just 233 matches. Only Roger Hunt (226) reached the milestone in fewer games. Luis Diaz scored his first goal for the club.

v Leeds United
Wednesday, February 23rd, 7.45pm

‘I CAN’T IMAGINE WHAT IT WOULD HAVE BEEN LIKE TO TRY AND DO ALL THIS WITHOUT JAMES’

Premier League

February 2022

GOOD evening and welcome back to Anfield for our Premier League fixture against Leeds United. I welcome Marcelo Bielsa, his players, staff, officials and the supporters of our visitors.

You know exactly what to expect from a team managed by Marcelo. They will be brave, industrious, streetwise, innovative and relentless. This Leeds absolutely reflects the beliefs of their leader.

Every game we have played against them, since they came back to the top-flight under Marcelo's stewardship, has been so intense. That's what they bring. They bring the intensity. So we have to be ready not just to match it, but to exceed it.

There is no question Marcelo and his staff have faced challenges this season, particularly with injury. But they are very much back in a positive mood and I think what they do in this moment makes them extremely dangerous.

My respect and admiration for their manager could not be higher. He has guru status in the game and it's well-earned. So many coaches look up to him. It's because he always has a clear plan. A clear idea. He knows what he wants.

I am writing this column prior to their fixture over the weekend against Manchester United, so I don't have any information from that contest to reflect on. But I can from ours.

The win over Norwich City was important for us, because we did it in quite stressful circumstances. I don't mean 'stress' in the mental sense by the way, more physical and environmental.

We only arrived back from Milan on Thursday afternoon and were kicking off again on Saturday at 3pm. That is not an excuse, it's just information and fact.

It meant we went into the match with just one training session to prepare. We had to make changes, that much was obvious. So for the team to navigate the contest as they did, with so many of that line-up having such little prep time, it was really cool, to be honest.

I think it was around seven changes to the starting positions we made and every player who came in showed they have embraced the most important mindset of this squad: be ready to contribute.

We have been blessed with stability in recent weeks but the flip-side of that means we have top players, training at the highest level, not getting the game-time their talent and application truly deserves. To be able to deal with that and then come in and put in an accomplished performance when required takes an elite mentality. We are blessed with it.

At the time of writing this I haven't conducted my pre-match press duties to preview the Leeds game, but I don't need to have fortune-telling powers to guess it would have been about the state of the title race and asking about what is possible for this team to achieve.

Sometimes I might appear snappy when answering those sorts of questions and in those moments I wish I was a little more patient maybe.

But the exasperation comes from the fact that talking about something speculatively, particularly as a participant, is entirely futile.

Us saying what we think could happen doesn't help it happen. Us ruling something out from happening equally doesn't make it so. The only 'achievement' we can talk about in the here-and-now is what we can control. Tonight it's about trying to win a game of football against Leeds United. That's the only mountain we can scale and it's a tough one to conquer.

We can't win anything tonight other than three league points, if we are fortunate enough to do so. The only thing we can lose tonight is the opportunity to add more points to our total. That's it. The beginning and the end.

And it's why the only game that matters for a team with a proper mentality is the next one you play. What your rivals and opponents do is out of our control, so conjecture over that is pointless for those of us tasked with delivering.

When I say all this, I try to make a point which applies to us as a team, management and staff only. It doesn't apply to supporters or even the media. Fans should always dream and if that means getting swept up in the moment, in a positive manner, then really cool. The 'what ifs' are also fine for those who write, broadcast and comment on the game.

But we can't afford to live in that world, otherwise we risk losing focus.

We love to win and we treat each win as special. But then it's done. The wider context at this stage isn't interesting to us. Our life is a series of mountains to climb. Each matchday we are back at base-camp and we hope to reach a new summit again.

So I apologise in advance for a series of repetitive and boring answers in press conferences and interviews if asked what I think is 'possible'. This will apply after setbacks as much as it does after achievements. Personally speaking, I think the games themselves are enough reason for joy and anticipation. This game tonight is one which sets the pulses racing on its own, without broader context or motivation required. Trying to beat Leeds this evening is all the motivation we need to show up and give our all. I'm sure it's the same for our supporters.

Given who we play tonight, there is one individual from our ranks I want to focus on in this column. At Inter Milan, James Milner made his 800th senior club appearance.

It's fitting that this evening we face the club who gave him the first of those.

Leeds is a place and a club very close to his heart. I know he has affection and appreciation for all the organisations he has represented during two decades as a professional. However, it struck me looking at the breakdown of his 800 that Liverpool was the club he'd played for the most.

What he does for us is so valuable. And I make a point of keeping my language in the present tense because he continues to do it, day in and day out. He has been a constant during my time at LFC and I was thinking just the other day that I can't imagine what it would have been like to try and do all this without him here.

It's no secret James is in the last year of his current deal – and again I emphasise 'current'. I spoke recently about 'talks' taking place to extend his stay with us and I thought it might make sense to use this platform to clarify that as I've seen some misleading reporting around it.

By talks I mean I have indicated my wish that James stays with us beyond this season, in a playing capacity. James will keep playing, he has told me this. So he should, by the way.

The level he is at, physically, technically and in terms of personal desire and hunger for more, means he should play on for as long as that lasts. I hope it will be here and that is what I have told those at the club who take on these tasks.

It's not fair or right to then jump to the conclusion that an offer has been made, because I don't think that's fair on James. I know I don't normally go into this much detail on matters such as this, but given how conscientious James is when it comes to not putting private things into the public domain, I wanted to make the actual position clear.

As should be the case, these things will get picked up in private and James will keep doing for us what he has done during my entire time working with him. He gives his all, he helps the collective and he sets the standards. We are very blessed to have him at our club.

Hopefully this evening can be another occasion at Anfield we all enjoy together. Terrific fixture. Under the lights. Exciting stage of the season. We can make it as special as we want it to be, collectively.

I hope we can do ourselves proud.

Liverpool 6, Leeds United 0

Goals: Salah (15pen, 35pen), Matip (30), Mane (80, 90), Van Dijk (90+3)

Line-up: Alisson, Alexander-Arnold, Matip, Van Dijk, Robertson, Jones (Milner 77), Fabinho, Thiago (Henderson 68), Salah, Mane, Diaz (Origi 85). Subs not used: Konate, Keita, Oxlade-Chamberlain, Minamino, Tsimikas, Kelleher

Jürgen's post-match reaction: 'The challenge we obviously face every week, but this week was especially difficult because Leeds play so different to all other teams, [is] when you then have only one proper session to prepare it. You saw in the game that we needed the first 15 minutes at least to get used to it properly. So, it was a hectic starting phase, a lot of pressing balls here, pressing balls when we could have calmed the game down, we didn't. But then we found our feet pretty much and then we really calmed the game down, then really our passing, our timing, everything was better. Positioning was better, movements were better and then we scored the goals. Forced the penalties obviously, but scored the goals. I thought the longer the game went, the better we used the size of the pitch and then with the way Leeds defend, it's then obviously really tricky to win all these one-on-one battles, all these kind of things. Then we scored really nice goals and could have scored even more. So, yes, very happy about the performance.'

Post-match notes

The six goals in this match took the Reds on to 70 Premier League goals for the season, two more than they managed in all 38 league matches the previous campaign.

ENERGY DRINK
18

'IT WAS REALLY NICE TO CELEBRATE WITH THE PEOPLE. I'M REALLY HAPPY ABOUT THE WHOLE THING'

Sunday, February 27th, 4.30pm
Carabao Cup final
Chelsea 0, Liverpool 0 aet

(Liverpool win 11-10 on penalties)

Penalty scorers: Milner, Fabinho, Van Dijk, Alexander-Arnold, Salah, Jota, Origi, Robertson, Elliott, Konate, Kelleher

Line-up: Kelleher, Alexander-Arnold, Matip (Konate 91), Van Dijk, Robertson, Henderson (Elliott 79), Fabinho, Keita (Milner 80), Salah, Mane (Jota 80), Diaz (Origi 97). Subs not used: Alisson, Oxlade-Chamberlain, Minamino, Tsimikas

Post-match notes

Following 21 successful penalties from both teams, Kepa Arrizabalaga's miss meant the Reds lifted the League Cup for a record ninth time.

Jürgen's post-match reaction:

On whether it was the perfect way to win the trophy because 'everyone contributed'...

"Perfect would have been if we could have had more players on the teamsheet already. Today I had to make a few really tough decisions and I said [to] the boys in the meeting when all the boys were in – even the boys who were not on the teamsheet – that, 'This here is my squad.' Plus – and now I have to be careful that I don't forget anybody – Tyler Morton, who was not with us in the hotel because he's slightly injured, Conor, Owen, Harvey from the U18s, Elijah played some minutes as well, Adrian saved us in Preston. The whole journey was absolutely outstanding. We had Adrian at Preston and then we scored the two goals. Without Takumi and without Divock and the goals they scored in the competition, we would not be here. So then we were 3-1 down against Leicester, I think most of the people wrote us off in that moment, so we came back – wonderful story, penalty shoot-out, won it. Then we had to change the away and the home game with Arsenal – 0-0 at home against 10 men, nobody was really positive about the second leg and we went there and won in a really nice manner.

And now tonight, facing Chelsea, there was like two lions going for each other – it was absolutely crazy. They started better, we took over and were then better. Second half, started again with two really good moments of Chelsea, we sorted it again and then in the end everybody was tired on the pitch obviously and then you have to get through. Then the penalty shoot-out, one of the most spectacular I ever saw. Absolutely great to win it like this. We called it the people's cup but the whole journey was a squad journey and that's what I love most about it."

On how his relationship has grown with Caoimhin Kelleher...

"Is it only the last four years? So I don't know when I saw Caoimhin the first time but it's true, it's quite a journey from when I saw him the first time, from the boy I saw the first time to the man he is today. I saw from the first second that he is an incredible talent. First John Achterberg, then Jack Robinson joined us since then as well, the boys are very, very positive. And if you know how a football team works and you know that goalies are very often separate, so I don't see them all the time but I see them in decisive moments. So, the development is absolutely top-class. Alisson Becker is the best goalie in the world, for me. There are goalies out there but this goalie is absolutely insane. But to be 100 per cent honest, for me Caoimhin Kelleher is the best No.2 in the world as well, especially for the way we play.

He had an incredible game. People asked me rightly two weeks ago or something if we will give Caoimhin another game to get some rhythm or whatever. To be 100 per cent honest, it was the first time I thought about it, 'Yeah, he has rhythm.' But that's the life of a No.2, especially for a young No.2, that you just have to be ready when you are called. The game he played tonight was absolutely incredible. I'm not 100 per cent sure I have the full story of the whole game but I can remember at least two incredible saves – probably there were more. So, he proved that the decision to line him up was absolutely right. And then in a very spectacular penalty shoot-out, he showed the whole range of his skillset. First and foremost, he's a goalkeeper but he finished one off with his really skilled feet. Top-class."

On the feeling and momentum this trophy win will provide with so much still to play for this season…

"So, it's good. Look, we were here and lost a final in a penalty shoot-out like six, seven years ago. Afterwards nobody talks about it, it's like, 'You were twice at Wembley and you lost both finals'. It was a tight game, we were clearly better in the second half against Man City that time. We should have won it in the second half, didn't, and then in the shoot-out we lose 4-1. They scored with all of them I think, we missed one, I'm not 100 per cent sure anymore. That's life. As a professional sportsperson, that's life. So now, in 10 years' time, nobody will ask, 'How did you win exactly against Chelsea?' You just have to win it. Were we better tonight than that time against City? I'm not 100 per cent sure, to be honest, but we are more experienced, that's a massive difference. We don't get nervous when things don't go well. We keep really our nerve and stuff like this.

How I said, the start of the game was clearly better

from Chelsea but all of a sudden, we were really in the game and then we let them run and we were the clear dominant team. I'm not sure 100 per cent but the first half was like 63 or something [per cent] possession – against Chelsea that's not that easy, so there was a lot of good football stuff obviously. But over 120 minutes you cannot hold them back and away from your goal, so they had their chances and obviously they scored 'goals' more than us, but they all were offside. That's pretty harsh to take for them I can imagine but I'm really happy about the effort and all these kind of things and yes, it's a big one for us because it's the first time for this group but the ninth time for the club, which is very important as well.

Our fans were obviously quite happy about the whole thing tonight, the atmosphere was outstanding, I really loved it. And after the game it was nice to celebrate with the people after a long time without having any reason to celebrate something, or not the opportunity to celebrate something. So, I'm really happy about the whole thing."

The players' post-match reaction:

Caoimhin Kelleher:

"Someone said to me afterwards, 'You scored the winning penalty' but I wasn't really bothered about that and I was more bothered that I wanted to make a save! But, thank God, anyway I scored and we got the win.

I was dreaming good things last night, that we would win, but never in my wildest dreams would I have thought I'd score a penalty at the Liverpool end, the winning penalty. That's just next level.

He [Alisson] is brilliant. You saw Chelsea change their goalkeeper at the end as well, so for me to get the faith from the manager was special and Ali has just been great with me. There was no sulking or anything like that, he's totally focused and he has been really helpful for me."

Jordan Henderson:

"It's very special to win trophies for this football club, no matter what the competition. It was a great opportunity for us and thankfully we were on the right side of it. It's always difficult when it goes to penalties; it's never nice. But I thought the lads deserved to win overall.

It's really pleasing that we've used all of the squad from the start of the competition – players from the first team and academy have all chipped in, which makes it even more special.

I never take for granted playing for this football club and how special that is – and to be winning trophies is extra special. The fans deserve it, the players deserve it. It was a fantastic day and hopefully this can give us a little kick-start for the last few months of the season because there's a lot of football to be played."

Andy Robertson:
"I was desperate for him [Kelleher] to save one, especially when I knew mine was coming up. I was so desperate for him to save one! His pen was ridiculous. That's where I think penalty shoot-outs are horrible – when it gets to the end it's lads that are the least confident and don't really want to take one and they sometimes decide the finals. But Caoimh's penalty was different class. The most important thing was we won it, whatever way we were willing to do it, whatever way possible. It had to go to penalties and luckily we all scored ours.

It has been really tight between us and Chelsea all season. The two games in the Premier League have both been draws. Today, we both had chances; I think they probably had the better chances, to be honest with you. Quite an open game, but I think by the end everyone was just knackered and I think you could just see both sets of teams were kind of looking at each other thinking, 'When will this end?' It's really tough on the body, a lot of work has been put into this. The longer it goes, somebody has to miss a penalty and it's horrible really. But, fortunately, it wasn't one of our lads."

Virgil van Dijk:
"The games we've played against Chelsea have always been very intense so it was expected but we're just very

happy that we got the trophy. It gives us something to build on for the rest of the season.

There were outstanding penalties from all of us. Under full pressure everyone did well. We practised them quite a bit.

At Liverpool we are all a family and we do things together. The atmosphere today was outstanding and we're all very happy. Credit to all the players who have been involved, from the youngsters who started the competition to the players who haven't played as much of the league campaign – so everyone has been a part of this.

I'm very happy for Caoimhin. It will give him a boost of confidence and it will make him more mature to play the way he played at this level."

MAR

2022

With one trophy safely in the cabinet, the Reds kept alive their hopes of adding to the haul of silverware, winning all three Premier League games, overcoming tricky opponents in the FA Cup and reaching the quarter-finals of the Champions League

2nd: Norwich City (FA) H
5th: West Ham (PL) H
8th: Internazionale (CL) H
12th: Brighton (PL) A
16th: Arsenal (PL) A
20th: Nottingham Forest (FA) A

March 2022

v Norwich City
Wednesday, March 2nd, 8.15pm

'YOU DON'T GET TO PICK UP THE TROPHY WITHOUT CRUCIAL CONTRIBUTIONS IN EARLIER ROUNDS'

FA Cup fifth round

Jürgen Klopp

GOOD evening and welcome back to Anfield for our FA Cup match against Norwich City.

I welcome Dean Smith, his players, staff, officials and the supporters of our visitors.

It was only a couple of weeks ago we faced each other here in the Premier League, so I don't need to repeat all I wrote about Dean that day. Nothing has changed since. I still think he is an outstanding leader of his team and club. A really good person as well with a top family. One of football's good guys without doubt.

We learned in our last game how strong they are. We needed some luck and magic moments to get through. They were in front in the game and were absolutely in every moment. We might both have different starting 11s tonight – or at least some changes – but I think the contest will be similar. Two honest and committed teams. Two teams going all out for the win. Two teams who will give their all.

It's a different competition tonight but I'm sure the same level of intensity will be there. The quarter-final awaits the winner, so it's a serious stage. We both have lots to do in the Premier League still but for this evening none of that matters. The only thing that matters tonight is this contest. And we throw ourselves into it.

Of course I cannot ignore what happened on Sunday, although it doesn't help or hinder us tonight. We played 120 minutes, plus pens – and therefore that's relevant information. It means we probably will have to factor that into team selection at least, but we would anyway.

The Carabao Cup win was something special for all of us. There are so many parts of it that make me burst with happiness.

Firstly because it really is the competition which encompasses the entire squad, including our young players. This cup is all about the journey. You don't get to pick up the trophy at Wembley without the crucial contributions in the earlier rounds. These games come in a part of the season where the demands on the team are crazy. Premier League games, Champions League games and international football. So everyone has to contribute and play their part. Without everyone we have no chance.

The worst part of my job is disappointing people who don't deserve it. When selecting a squad in the circumstances we had to on Sunday, this was so hard. But the truth is even without being on the team sheet for the final, the win is still just as much about them and what they did for us and this club. It's not the best comparison, but when you win a league title it's not just the players who feature in the final match day who are considered champions. It's everyone. Same with the League Cup on Sunday. We won it because of what happened at Norwich away, Preston away, Leicester at Anfield and over two games against Arsenal.

The other part that made Sunday incredible was being able to celebrate it with our supporters. The Liverpool section of Wembley… wow! And I mean wow! The atmosphere was one I will remember for the rest of my life. And it was constant. They were with us for every second of it. And then after… that felt like a party.

I am so pleased we can again have these moments. The world still encounters truly awful things, but at least on Sunday, inside Wembley, we were able to have a shared experience which was all about joy.

I must admit it was a strange feeling in the build-up to the game. I have said previously that before we played Atletico Madrid in March 2020 it was an occasion when my mind was not entirely on football. It wasn't quite the same this week, but it wasn't far from it.

What Ukraine is subjected to in this moment is one of the most distressing things in my lifetime. I have a lot of friends who are from this amazing country. We, as a club, were in the great city of Kyiv as recently as 2018 for the Champions League final. What a welcome we were given! What hospitality and generosity we were shown!

To see those same streets and landmarks now under attack, unprovoked attack, is heart-breaking. It's too much to bear at times.

I am not a politician or a diplomat and I know my words will count for nothing, but I pray each hour of the day that this madness stops and stops before any more innocent people lose their lives. I have spent time in Russia also in my career and know Russian people; they are people with love in their hearts. This is not representative of them. It is not in their name. Showing support for Ukraine is separate. To support Ukraine now is about supporting humanity against brutality.

So yes, continuing to prepare and play football matches against this backdrop isn't easy but it is the job to do. And as Sunday showed, football still gives us the opportunity to present the best of ourselves and find joy in something that is about the collective and community.

Coming back to tonight, I don't know what team we will select, but I know we approach the game with the only motivation being to win and get through. Norwich will have the same objective. So it's a proper game.

Under the lights at Anfield. I'm sure there will still be a feelgood factor for the supporters because of Sunday. That's cool. I don't discourage that.

For us, we cannot allow any 'follow over' other than a feeling of positivity and greed for more. I want us, as a team, to be completely in tonight and nothing else. The trophy we have won won't matter come kick-off. The trophies we could still win are irrelevant right now. The only thing that can be achieved tonight is progression in the FA Cup. So let's do it. Let's have a right go, tonight, in this game. Let's make the performance and the atmosphere special. Really special. We can if we are minded to.

Liverpool 2, Norwich City 1

Goals: Minamino (27, 39)

Line-up: Alisson, Milner, Konate, Gomez, Tsimikas, Oxlade-Chamberlain, Henderson (Morton 61), Jones (Elliott 46), Minamino, Origi (Mane 84), Jota (Diaz 84). Subs not used: Adrian, Robertson, Matip, Kelleher, Bradley

Jürgen's post-match reaction: 'We had to make 10 changes because of the 120 plus 40 minutes penalty shoot-out on Sunday. That was an exhausting night, mentally and physically, so we had to make changes to have a chance tonight. We needed a couple of minutes to get into the game, Norwich had kind of a kickstart again like they had in the Premier League game. But from a specific moment on we controlled the game and played like we had to play. Taki's impression was obvious with scoring two goals and not only that – he had a lot more top, top football moments. He was a constant threat tonight, he was mobile, he was quick. He was technically on an incredibly high level.'

Post-match notes

Takumi Minamino became only the third Liverpool player to score against the same club in both domestic cups in the same season after Kenny Dalglish (1977/78 v Chelsea) and Luis Suarez (2011/12 v Stoke City).

March 2022

v West Ham
Saturday, March 5th, 5.30pm

'THE MORE PACKED THE CALENDAR IS AT THIS STAGE, THE MORE YOU HAVE TO PLAY FOR'

Premier League

Jürgen Klopp

GOOD afternoon and welcome back to Anfield for our Premier League fixture against West Ham United.

I welcome David Moyes, his players, staff, officials and the supporters of our visitors.

What a season West Ham are having! Absolutely brilliant! David is a superb manager. It's hard to understate how highly he's respected by all of us who also do this job in England. He's smart and he sets his teams up really well while still giving them freedom and licence to express themselves.

When you prepare to face a team led by David, you know you are in for a really tough afternoon.

At the moment he would be a very strong contender for 'Manager of the Season', I would say. He has created an exceptional team there.

In the meeting we have already had this season they came out on top, so we have a very personal reminder for how dangerous and ruthless they can be. We don't need painful memories to make sure we are ready, but it is there nonetheless.

What is clear is we are facing them in a period where they have everything to play for. They are chasing teams like us for the top four and a chance of Champions League football. As we know all too well ourselves, to achieve that you have to keep winning. In this moment they are showing all the qualities you would require. That's great for them and so a big test for us.

Both of us played midweek in the FA Cup, but I'm not sure the outcome of either game will be much of an influence today. It means we have had similar recovery periods I suppose. But the results won't play a part.

For us, Wednesday is done with until we play in that competition again. For our opponent today they have the highest motivation possible to get a result and keep their Premier League momentum going.

I'm worried my programme notes could become even more repetitive than normal in the coming weeks and months, with one message in particular being resounding.

The only game of our season that matters is the next one. All that matters today is today. Yesterday is merely information and tomorrow we think about when it arrives. In football terms, of course.

I think during my time managing in England one of the things that strikes me most is how much focus there is on what 'could' be achieved while you are still in the process of trying to do it.

We speak so much about the 'what ifs'. I have my own 'what if'... What if we just try and enjoy being in every moment. Focus entirely on the now. Rather than thinking about the implications a result could have for something else further down the track, we just attack the match right in front of us. Immerse ourselves in it completely.

It has to be our mindset internally and the good news for me is that the players and staff at the AXA Training Centre are already there.

We prepare for each game like it is a final. Honestly, that's what we do. Yes, this period we are in is incredibly intense in terms of the sheer number of fixtures. Incidentally, we hope that doesn't change between now and May. We don't want it to. The more packed the calendar is at this stage, the more you have to play for.

But at the moment we play very often, which means the turnaround is swift. No sooner have you finished one contest than you are preparing for the next. I think this helps when it comes to focus actually. We cannot afford ourselves distraction – we don't have time for it.

My admiration for the players could not be higher in how they handle and approach things. No fuss, no drama, no excuses. Always ready. They are so low-maintenance as a group. They are the best self-regulators you could imagine. What they expect of themselves is higher than anything we could set for them. And as a manager that is such a blessing.

Another is seeing the way the club has campaigned to make LFC the most diverse and inclusive family we can be, something that is being celebrated at today's 'Red Together' fixture.

I have said before that being together always makes us stronger and it makes me incredibly proud that the club embraces these principles wholeheartedly. Seeing the diversity of our players, supporters and other staff at the club is what helps to make LFC so special.

It's vital that we all continue to play our part in the fight for equality in football and also within our wider society. The club takes its responsibility to talk about important issues and fight against all forms of discrimination very seriously.

Red Together is key to that commitment to equality, diversity and inclusion and that sense of togetherness allows us to enjoy every victory and every success all the more.

I mentioned earlier that Wednesday night won't be an influencing factor for the two teams when kick-off comes around today, but for our supporters though I hope it is.

When the programme of games is relentless, the impact of our home crowd is even more valuable. The energy they can give is critical to us as we saw against Norwich.

I know that we can count on our fans to drive us forward again this afternoon and hopefully we can enjoy another good day together.

Liverpool 1, West Ham 0

Goal: Mane (27)

Line-up: Alisson, Alexander-Arnold, Konate, Van

Dijk, Robertson, Henderson, Fabinho, Keita (Milner 90), Salah (Jota 79), Mane, Diaz (Jones 90+6). Subs not used: Gomez, Oxlade-Chamberlain, Minamino, Origi, Kelleher, Elliott

Jürgen's post-match reaction: 'You cannot only win the ones where you are flying. Today we were obviously not flying, we had to dig really deep and that's what the boys did. It is necessary to get something out of this season that we keep on going and [there is] no time to rest, so just keep going. The boys have now really proper quality in depth, but we cannot play all competitions and go far in the competitions if we don't have this depth, there is no chance. You can do it for a year when you are lucky with injuries, but I think we had years where Bobby, Sadio and Mo played pretty much all the games, if I am right. Sometimes they came from the bench, but the next game they started again. In a week, especially like this – Sunday, Wednesday, Saturday and Tuesday, when we play again against Inter – there is no chance that you try to get through with the same line-up.'

Post-match notes

Trent Alexander-Arnold reached a new personal best of 16 assists for the season in setting up Sadio Mane's winner. This was the Reds' 12th win in a row across all competitions.

March 2022

v Internazionale
Tuesday, March 8th, 8pm

'WORK HARD NOT JUST FOR YOUR OWN REWARDS, BUT FOR THE ENTIRE TEAM'S'

UEFA Champions League round of 16, second leg

GOOD evening and welcome back to Anfield for our UEFA Champions League tie against Inter Milan. I welcome Simone Inzaghi, his players, staff, officials and the supporters of our visitors.

What a fixture, hey? Even saying it out loud makes you excited. Liverpool versus Internazionale in the European Cup.

What makes it better is we face each other in a moment where we are both proper forces in the game. This isn't to sound arrogant about ourselves, by the way, I just think the current standings and performances of recent seasons makes this true. We are a proper team. For Inter, it is absolutely the case also. They are the real deal. They are a proper contender for this title.

What a job Simone is doing with this club! Current champions of Italy, near the top of Serie A again and looking very strong.

We watched their match on Friday night in the team hotel, ahead of our own game against West Ham. I don't see many weaknesses in them if I'm being honest. From back to front they have top-quality players, organised superbly well. A clear plan, a clear idea.

There is so much to like about how they play. I really enjoy watching them. Not so much having to face them, though.

The first leg in Milan was such a tough game. I would go so far as to say it was one of the most difficult of the season for us in all competitions. They were aggressive, in the positive sense of that word, and purposeful. We played very well and defended very well, which is why we come into this contest with an advantage in the tie.

But it is just an advantage at this stage and it means nothing if we don't have the right attitude coming into this one. It is only half-time. That is all. And if my team were trailing 2-0 at half-time my mindset would be game on, all to play for. Add in the fact they have 90 minutes and not 45, it is obvious we have a proper fight on our hands.

It is so important that everyone inside this stadium tonight, with Liverpool in their hearts, is ready to give all they have to ensure we progress in this competition. This is players, management and supporters. If anyone has even a tiny percentage of complacency or entitlement, please stay away.

We face a ruthless team, with elite mindset players, used to winning, with know-how of how to do what it takes in this competition and with a manager who is exceptional at building a plan to complete a job. Anyone who watched the first leg knows this also. This tie is alive and it is there to be attacked and won.

Our mindset, as a team or club, does not worry me for one second, for what it's worth. I only say all this because this is what this column is for: essentially to lay out the themes that matter to us going into a fixture.

Values matter to me, as the leader of this team and club.

Recently I have spoken a lot about focus and intensity. On Saturday I think we showed all the hallmarks of one of our most valuable traits: humility. Without humility in our approach, we have no chance.

West Ham were a proper threat. They are a top team this season. They came and they played really well. But we were not to be beaten because we had the humility to recognise that to win a contest against a side like that, you have to be prepared to work even harder than them.

They wanted it like crazy, but we wanted it even more. We didn't just want it in our minds – we wanted it in our sprinting, our pressing, our relentlessness, our resilience. And maybe most important of all, the acknowledgement that the importance of the collective always outweighs individual contribution. That's so critical for us. Work hard not just for your own rewards but for the entire team's. Sacrifice for the group.

I am biased, but I believe our individual quality is not to question. Throughout the entire squad, we have players with ability and talent by the bucket-load. But that's not enough on its own at this level. All your opponents have this also. It's absolutely not enough on its own if you want to be in the conversation and competing for special things consistently.

What I loved about the weekend's win was how much

we recognised, pretty much from the first whistle, that we would only be able to do the job and secure the points if we were prepared to battle and sacrifice.

We showed the mindset that to win the match you first have to win a fight and suffer for your team. Trust me, as a coach or manager you get more satisfaction from those sort of moments than the ones that make highlight reels.

As a case-study for this I want to point to Trent's performance against West Ham. After the game I was asked a lot about him because of his assist for the goal. The graphics on the TV and social media all focused on this also because his and Robbo's numbers are insane.

But to be honest, as nice as that is, it wasn't the thing that gave me the most pride from how he played. It never is. It was his tenacity to defend and win possession back for the team that was far more important.

Maybe I can't show it as much because the game is flowing and constant – and I am in it – but I honestly view the players doing those 'dirty' jobs with just as much pleasure as a moment of magic or genius.

A player sprinting to close down space, covering for a team-mate, being brave in a challenge, constantly making themselves available regardless of whether they will receive the ball or not to create more opportunities elsewhere on the pitch.

These are the real highlights, even though they

won't be made into a montage for the post-match TV discussions.

We have to constantly lean into these qualities. We are doing that at the moment and that's really cool.

I have no idea what the outcome will be in this tie, the competition as a whole or the other things we play for. And, at the moment, I couldn't care less. I only care about these 90 minutes, or 120 minutes, or 120 minutes plus penalty-kicks, whatever the evening brings us.

If we stay humble in our approach – by recognising skill alone, even in abundance, isn't enough, or allowing the misguided thought that individual brilliance alone will be a deciding factor – then we have a proper chance in every game we go into. And that will always be enough for me.

Finally, I opened these notes by saying what a special feeling this fixture creates, simply by seeing the two club names paired with each other. One of the biggest factors in that is atmosphere. When you think of Liverpool v Inter you think of a full and passionate Anfield. You think of it being electric and partisan.

Our supporters need no team-talk for a fixture with this heritage. This special place will be a cauldron of energy tonight, I'm sure. And we will need it.

If we all arrive knowing that to enjoy a special night we have to be our best and work our hardest, I am confident we can create more memories together.

Liverpool 0 Internazionale 1

(Liverpool win 2-1 on aggregate)

Line-up: Alisson, Alexander-Arnold, Matip, Van Dijk, Robertson, Jones (Keïta 65), Fabinho, Thiago (Henderson 65), Salah, Jota (Diaz 83), Mane. Subs not used: Milner, Gomez, Adrian, Oxlade-Chamberlain, Minamino, Tsimikas, Origi, Kelleher, Elliott

Jürgen's post-match reaction: 'Pete Krawietz always says the art of football is to lose the right games. I still hate it but if there was any kind of game we could have afforded to lose, it was tonight. But it's not that I'm here like over the moon. I'm really happy that we went through because obviously when we saw the draw in the first place it was like, 'Okay, that's a tough one.' So we went through and I think over the two legs we deserved it. When I think about the game, I didn't like our counter-press, I don't think we won any kind of ball back in the first 20 minutes. You have to be expansive when you are in possession, but when you lose the ball – and we lost the ball in strange moments – you have to chase the situation. But in the end, we have to respect the quality of the opponent. Now let's carry on.'

Post-match notes

This was Liverpool's first loss of 2022, though they still qualified for the quarter-finals on aggregate. The Reds hit the woodwork three times. They were unbeaten in their previous 28 home matches in all competitions.

Saturday, March 12th, 12.30pm
Premier League
Brighton 0, Liverpool 2

Goals: Diaz (19), Salah (61pen)

Line-up: Alisson, Alexander-Arnold, Matip, Van Dijk, Robertson, Henderson (Milner 86), Fabinho, Keita (Thiago 65), Salah (Jota 65), Mane, Diaz. Subs not used: Firmino, Gomez, Jones, Tsimikas, Kelleher, Elliott

Jürgen's post-match reaction: 'Difficult game, good opponent, we needed a few minutes to settle into the game. From the moment when we found ourselves in the game, we controlled it in a really good way. I don't think you can deny Brighton constantly or completely because of the quality they have, but we did quite well and scored a wonderful goal in a really good situation. Luis did what a striker had to do. I didn't see it back but it was spectacular enough in the first moment. To get in there with his head it was really brave. A great goal. Everybody asked me today was it a red card or not? You know if you get these questions, you know most of the people think it was a red card. We could have scored more, won good balls, real chances from open-play situations or counter-attacking moments, or both. I liked that a lot and I don't expect us to be two or three-nil up or whatever at Brighton. I really respect Brighton too much, so fine for half-time. We showed the boys a few situations – how we have to play, how we have to defend them. We expect them to change formation maybe again, that's what they usually do against us. The second half started again with a situation for Brighton but then after that we controlled it again, scored the second goal and in the last few minutes, they had a chance. Ali is a world-class goalie but from my understanding he should not have to show that in each game. He showed it again and that's good, that's why we have a clean sheet. I think we deserved the three points and that's actually all I am interested in. I am happy about most of the things.'

Post-match notes

Mo Salah's goal was his 20th league goal of the season and the Reds' 2,000th Premier League goal.

Wednesday, March 16th, 8.15pm
Premier League
Arsenal 0, Liverpool 2

Goals: Jota (54), Firmino (62)

Line-up: Alisson, Alexander-Arnold, Matip, Van Dijk, Robertson, Henderson, Fabinho, Thiago (Jones 90), Mane, Jota (Firmino 56), Diaz (Salah 56). Subs not used: Konate, Keita, Gomez, Oxlade-Chamberlain, Minamino, Kelleher

Jürgen's post-match reaction: 'I think we had six games more than Arsenal [since the Carabao Cup semi-final], you can see that… we constantly travel, we go here, we go there, we are in the hotel and stuff like this. Actually, I don't complain, we don't complain, it's just how it is. That's why I am so happy today obviously because coming here to Arsenal in that moment, against this team, winning 2-0, that's really special. That's really special. Of course it gives momentum but momentum is the most fragile flower on the planet: somebody just walks past you and steps on it and done and then you work again for I don't know how long to get momentum back.'

Post-match notes

The Reds recorded their ninth league win in a row to move just one point behind Manchester City at the top.

Sunday, March 20th, 6pm
FA Cup sixth round
Nottingham Forest 0, Liverpool 1

Goal: Jota (78)

Line-up: Alisson, Gomez, Konate, Van Dijk, Tsimikas, Keita (Henderson 64), Fabinho (Thiago 64), Oxlade-Chamberlain (Diaz 64), Elliott (Minamino 64), Firmino, Jota. Subs not used: Adrian, Jones, Origi, Matip, Beck

Jürgen's post-match reaction: 'It was the game we expected, especially if you don't use the chances and don't play as good as we could have done. We could have obviously played better, but we should have scored in the first half. If you score earlier it is a completely different game. If you score late-ish then Steve [Cooper] had obviously changed [tactics], very offensive, full risk and we had our counter-attacking chances, didn't use them, didn't play them out properly and it was 1-0 until the end. In cup competitions we all know there is only one reason to be part of it and that's to go to the next round. We were prepared for a fight, we came through it and I'm really happy about that.'

Post-match notes

Diogo Jota's goal was his 19th of the season – his best return in a single campaign. The Reds reached the FA Cup semi-final for the first time under Jürgen Klopp.

APR

2022

With the finishing line in sight, every game was a huge one, especially with Manchester City providing the opposition twice, plus games against Manchester United and Everton. And Jürgen had a nice surprise up his sleeve for everyone too...

2nd: Watford (PL) H
5th: Benfica (CL) A
10th: Manchester City (PL) A
13th: Benfica (CL) H
16th: Manchester City (FA) N
19th: Manchester United (PL) H
24th: Everton (PL) H
27th: Villarreal (CL) H
30th: Newcastle (PL) A

April 2022

v Watford
Saturday, April 2nd, 12.30pm

'I'M BUZZING TO HAVE SUPPORTERS HERE FOR THE JOURNEY, NOT JUST THE DESTINATION'

Premier League

Jürgen Klopp

GOOD afternoon and welcome to Anfield for our Premier League fixture against Watford. I welcome Roy Hodgson, his players, staff, officials and the supporters of our visitors. Firstly, can I say what a joyful surprise it is to have Roy back in the dugout. We were the opponents for his last match as Crystal Palace manager here, the final game of last season.

I remember his words acutely. It was very much, "I am calling it a day…maybe!" The "maybe" was loud and clear.

I could tell there was still so much more left inside him. I'm not saying he didn't mean it, of course. It's just that I think it was always going to take something appropriate for him and Watford fits the bill.

They are very fortunate to have him and Ray Lewington, his assistant, I think. As a management team they are experienced and have a track record of what Watford need right now. They make teams organised, hard to play against and really hard to beat. For teams fighting for their lives, being hard to beat is definitely the best possible trait.

Watford have proved this season that on their day they can better any opponent. We have to be ready for this. They have the highest motivation possible: playing for their survival. They will come with a plan and belief. It will be real work. But we are no strangers to this, so let's go!

This game kicks off a remarkable period for us as a club but it's never been more important to focus only on what is directly in front of us.

Hopefully there are no unforeseen reasons for a break between now and the end of the season, so it's a sprint finish in all competitions. The fact we already view each match as a final means we don't have to adjust our mindset – we only need to maintain the focus we already have.

During the international break, I had the opportunity to think back to the start of the season and some of the thoughts and hopes we shared. One of those was arriving into the situation we find ourselves in now. A situation packed with opportunity.

That's what we've given ourselves. A real chance. And that's fantastic.

I'd have to check but I'm pretty sure it was the start of the campaign when I wrote about a comment I'd heard from a supporter which I really liked. It was that the phrase 'glory hunter' can often be tagged to those drawn to following certain clubs. The point was with Liverpool it's different. It's not 'glory hunting', it's 'journey hunting'. And I think this sentiment matters more today than at any point.

It is about the journey and we are on it. This shouldn't be twisted to suggest a specific destination either – I don't mean a specific target.

Let's get the perspective right here. We are in three competitions right now. I'm not a person who understands betting so I'm not sure what the odds are, but I doubt very much we are favourites in any? I'm sure we are not rank outsiders either, but for certain not an outright frontrunner. That's cool.

Also, it doesn't matter. Because it's the journey that will decide, not anyone's expectation or formula. I'm not sure if I have ever been the leader of a team who at the start of a competition was outright favourite to win it, but equally I couldn't care less. This fact has never made me fight harder to win. It wouldn't make me fight less, if the other way around.

Being journey hunters brings its own energy. It means you get to enjoy the moment and be in every moment. I can't think of a time when it's more important to channel this, than on days like today.

A lunchtime kick-off, after an international break against opposition fighting for their lives with a streetwise leader. All the ingredients to trip you up. It means focus has to be absolute, and not a focus on something that might happen – a focus only on today, the 90 minutes, nothing else.

When you are a team and club who takes maximum joy from the journey, like we do, days like this are so important. We recognise how tough the match is. We show the contest the respect it deserves, through our effort and our approach. We reflect humility by ensuring we give all we have. Maximum effort is required from everyone inside this ground who loves LFC.

Being able to embrace the thrill of the journey and realise it's where fulfilment comes, really matters. In my time at this football club I think we have done this so well as a collective. No entitlement ever. We fight so hard together, give so much together because we recognise how difficult it is to achieve these special moments.

I'm buzzing to be back at Anfield, with a full house of supporters who are here for the journey and not just the destination. It's why this stadium is always full of energy.

Today will be hard work. We have to fight with all we have because our opponent comes with their own expectation and their own objective.

As the team and management, we know total focus and complete commitment on today's task is our only concern and it's more than enough to make us energised.

I know it will be the same for the home sections of Anfield.

Let's take joy from the challenge.

Liverpool 2, Watford 0

Goals: Jota (22), Fabinho (89pen)

Line-up: Alisson, Gomez, Matip, Van Dijk, Robertson, Jones (Fabinho 62), Henderson, Thiago (Milner 90), Salah (Mane 69), Firmino, Jota.

Subs not used: Konate, Oxlade-Chamberlain, Tsimikas, Diaz, Kelleher, Alexander-Arnold

Jürgen's post-match reaction: 'These games can go either way; if you score early, really early, then just get in kind of a flow, it can go in one direction. But it's not very likely, it's really unlikely that after the international break you see the best game of the season. So we had to work through this game against a very well-organised Watford side. Roy is doing a really incredible job. After [going] 1-0 down, nothing changed, going for counter-attacks. When the players came on, going for counter-attacks. It makes it uncomfortable. We had in the first half obviously the one scary moment when Ali had this incredible save. But we scored our goal, nice, and kept it controlled, which is the most important thing. Scoring the second was obviously kind of a relief. Winning the game is all we wanted, the boys delivered and so now we can carry on.'

Post-match notes

Diogo Jota chalked up his 20th goal of the season in a win that briefly put the Reds top of the Premier League. It was Jürgen Klopp's side's 10th league win in a row.

Tuesday, April 5th, 8pm
UEFA Champions League quarter-final, first leg
Benfica 1, Liverpool 3

Goals: Konate (17), Mane (34), Diaz (87)

Line-up: Alisson, Alexander-Arnold (Gomez 89), Konate, Van Dijk, Robertson, Keita (Milner 89), Fabinho, Thiago (Henderson 61), Salah (Jota 61), Mane (Firmino 61), Diaz. Subs not used: Oxlade-Chamberlain, Jones, Minamino, Tsimikas, Matip, Kelleher, Elliott

Jürgen's post-match reaction: 'We came here for a result. I didn't expect the game being any easier, I knew. I have to say, big compliment to Benfica, they really fought for their lives, especially after we opened the door a little bit for them. It was clear when they scored that the crowd will be back and the atmosphere was really, really good. And good football teams tend to use that. But we could calm them down immediately a little bit with the three changes. I think it helped. The other boys worked really hard but they have all a tough period they're going through. That's why it was helpful that we could bring fresh legs. Then the game was slightly more open than I would have wished, of course, but we scored the third one and I think everybody agrees we could have scored more goals, maybe should have. How I said, big compliment to Benfica but anyway, the best player of Benfica was the goalie probably. That says a lot. It's half-time, we are two goals up. We were in half-time today two goals up and we knew it wasn't over. That's exactly the same information we have now. Now they have to come to Anfield and we have to use that.'

Post-match notes

Luis Diaz made his first Champions League start for the Reds and crowned the appearance with a crucial goal and assist.

April 2022

Sunday, April 10th, 4.30pm
Premier League
Manchester City 2, Liverpool 2

Goals: Jota (13), Mane (46)

Line-up: Alisson, Alexander-Arnold, Matip, Van Dijk, Robertson, Henderson (Keita 78), Fabinho, Thiago, Salah, Jota (Diaz 70), Mane (Firmino 84). Subs not used: Konate, Milner, Gomez, Jones, Tsimikas, Kelleher

Jürgen's post-match reaction: 'I think the support was, again, simply incredible. We could calm down the City crowd slightly with the football we played in moments, but there were other moments really on their toes. I liked the game, atmosphere-wise as well. Nothing changed, really. We have to be nearly perfect to beat this team in a game and over a season as well. We knew in January if we wanted to win it we have to win 18 games and if there is one we can draw it was today. We drew and now let's see. We have now two massive games for us: we have Benfica on Wednesday and City again Saturday and then after that it really starts, we have to be ready for our derbies.'

Post-match notes

Sadio Mane scored to make it 2-2 on his 30th birthday. The draw ended Liverpool's record run of eight straight away wins in all competitions.

v Benfica
Wednesday, April 13th, 8pm

'SADIO IS A MACHINE. WHAT HE HAS DONE PUTS HIM IN THE BRACKET OF 'LEGEND''

UEFA Champions League quarter-final, second leg

GOOD evening and welcome back to Anfield for our UEFA Champions League match against Benfica. I welcome Nelson Verissimo, his players, staff, officials and the supporters of our visitors.

I don't know Nelson that well personally, but it is clear having faced his team in Portugal in the first leg he is a fierce competitor. He is someone who knows the club inside-out and has done an exceptional job since taking over. The manner in which they knocked out Ajax in the previous round demonstrates how dangerous they are in this competition in particular.

We had huge respect for Benfica before we travelled there to face them last week, but that has only increased following the first-leg contest. Yes, the scoreline on the night was in our favour and we have an advantage. But anyone who watched the game, and certainly those of us competing directly in it, appreciate their quality and the danger they pose. There were periods where we had to show real resilience.

They are brave and smart. They are well-organised. They have a proper goal-threat.

I was conscious when starting this column that in some respects the messages within might be similar to when we faced Inter Milan at Anfield in the second leg of our last-16 tie. As with tonight, we arrived into the game with a two-goal lead. As with tonight, we knew the contest was far from over. And as with tonight, we knew there were at least 90 minutes in which both teams could fight to get to the next round. We knew all this ahead of the Inter Milan second leg and so it proved.

It was such a battle to get through. But that's how it should be. This is the best club competition in world sport. It's ferociously hard in each and every game and we expect it to be exactly the same this evening – if not even harder because we are a round further on.

Ahead of the first leg it struck me that to reach a UEFA Champions League quarter-final you need exceptional and committed players, who show a bravery in their approach and are humble enough to recognise that you have to work harder than your opponent if you want success. I think this applies to us for sure and then some. But Benfica also. They are a proper threat to us.

It's also true that the qualities you have to show, both collectively and as individuals, to reach the last eight are also required if you want to make a semi-final.

You can never assume. You can never feel entitled. It is not allowed. And this applies to every second of every game. Switch off in this competition and you are 'toast'. The history of this great tournament is littered with examples. Clubs and teams who are planning the next stage before a particular round is complete are inviting problems.

I think and I hope – actually I am certain – that as a team and club we do not have this complacency within us. We know this tie is alive. We know if we drop even the smallest percentage in our quality or commitment we will be watching the semi-finals on TV rather than having the privilege of playing in them.

So that is the clear message, for players, staff and supporters: if you come to Anfield tonight, come with anticipation yes, but the anticipation of having to win a battle to get through. Those of us blessed to be here need to show humility. We can do that by giving everything we have over the 90-plus minutes – and if it goes that way and it is needed – extra-time and penalties.

Benfica arrive into this game on the back of an excellent league win at the weekend. For us, it was a hugely intense game against Manchester City and a draw which on the day was probably a fair reflection of how it played out. There were tons of things I loved about the performance; other parts, not so much. But that is pretty standard for most games, win, lose or draw. Our effort could not be criticised. Nor our bravery. I love this.

Someone said afterwards that whenever Manchester City have led in matches this season they have always won. So the fact we came back not just once but twice is a reason to be positive. It shows our fighting qualities, our ability to strike back in the face of setbacks; that when under pressure, the most intense pressure possible, you can stay cool and react in the right way.

Everyone who played for us on the day contributed to an important result, but I did want to pick out Sadio. It was his 30th birthday on the day of the game and he still looks as fresh and vibrant as when he joined this club as a younger professional.

He is a machine. What he has done for this club and continues to do puts him in the bracket of 'legend'. For LFC and Senegal he is playing to his highest level possible.

What's exciting is how he is getting better and stronger. When you see how he looks after himself and his commitment to his profession, turning 30 for him really is only a number.

His attitude and character are elite. We are so appreciative of him and I know for sure the levels he reaches at the moment are not the peak – there is even more to come from this very special player.

Earlier I spoke about comparisons with the Inter Milan tie and I want to come back to that. One of the biggest factors that evening, in dragging us through an incredibly difficult tie, was the Anfield crowd.

Our supporters knew their job and they performed it perfectly. They gave us energy when we needed it. They gave us the power to get over the line. It really has to be the same tonight. Because we will need it 100 per cent.

Finally, on something that will always be more important to this club and this city than any football match, tonight we mark the anniversary of the Hillsborough tragedy.

When speaking on this subject I am woefully inadequate to find words that properly reflect its significance. I try to leave that to others. But I know – because I talk to people who understand far better than me – that taking time to remember and reflect around this time is so important to the families of the victims and the survivors.

For those who lost loved ones on that awful day, the pain will never diminish. For those who were there, who themselves were hurt or injured – or even witnessed the horror – they can never eradicate those feelings.

So we must continue to support them and observe this anniversary in a manner which honours the memory of those we lost. But also acknowledge the courage, fortitude and reliance of the people who fought for justice in their memory for decades.

The majority of us honoured to represent this club today can never truly comprehend the suffering, but we can express our love and our solidarity.

That is what we will do tonight and on 15 April itself.

Liverpool 3, Benfica 3

(Liverpool win 6-4 on aggregate)

Goals: Konate (21), Firmino (55, 65)

Line-up: Alisson, Gomez, Matip, Konate, Tsimikas, Keita,

Henderson (Fabinho 58), Milner (Thiago 58), Diaz (Mane 66), Firmino (Origi 90+1), Jota (Salah 57). Subs not used: Van Dijk, Oxlade-Chamberlain, Jones, Robertson, Kelleher, Alexander-Arnold, Elliott

Jürgen's post-match reaction: 'It never happened that I take something like this for granted. I'm really, really happy. That's it pretty much. I said it now a couple of times, I know we will talk about the game and the things that happened, the goals we conceded and all of these kind of things, but on a day when I'm not over the moon about qualifying for the Champions League semi-finals then something is really wrong – maybe it would be the right time just to quit. So, it's all good.'

Post-match notes

At the age of 36, James Milner became the oldest Englishman to start a Champions League match. Ibrahima Konate became the fourth LFC player to score in both legs of a Champions League quarter-final after Peter Crouch (2006/07), Mo Salah (2017/18) and Roberto Firmino (2018/19).

April 2022

Saturday, April 16th, 3.30pm
FA Cup semi-final
Manchester City 2, Liverpool 3

Goals: Konate (9), Mane (17, 45)

Line-up: Alisson, Alexander-Arnold, Konate, Van Dijk, Robertson, Keita (Henderson 73), Fabinho, Thiago (Jones 87), Salah, Mane (Jota 85), Diaz (Firmino 85). Subs not used: Milner, Gomez, Tsimikas, Matip, Kelleher

Jürgen's post-match reaction: 'He [Sadio] played an incredible game, an absolutely incredible game. He was the first player to start the press, so it was intense for him as well. The first goal he scored, I love it. The acceleration of Sadio, the desire to get there, it was really great. And the other one was proper football until the final pass with the little chip and then the volley – it was a great goal. Ibou scored now the third goal in his third start in a row, if I'm 100 per cent right, which is very helpful as well. Set-pieces are very important, especially [when] teams are a little bit more focused on Virgil, so it's really important that the second target player can use that. He did it three times, it's really cool.'

Post-match notes

Ibrahima Konate scored his third goal in his last three starts as the Reds reached their first FA Cup final during Jürgen Klopp's reign.

Jürgen Klopp

v Manchester United
Tuesday, April 19th, 8pm

'THE RIVALRY THAT EXISTS BETWEEN THE CLUBS IS SPECIAL. IT IS AN ENGLISH 'CLASICO''

Premier League

April 2022

IT was only a few weeks ago that I said every game for the rest of this season would be a final. To be honest, I didn't need to say that about tonight's fixture. If there is one game in our schedule which will always be a final, it is Liverpool versus Manchester United.

If ever a match needs zero build-up it is this one.

Just being involved in games like this is a privilege. The history of the two clubs and the rivalry that exists between them is so special that you don't even have to come from Liverpool or Manchester to be able to appreciate it.

I knew all about it when I lived and worked in Germany and the same goes for so many people around the world who love football. It is an English 'Clasico' in this respect.

If I was not fortunate enough to be manager of one of the two teams, I would want a ticket to watch Liverpool and United play against each other.

It would not matter what the competition is or how well the teams are performing, the intensity and the passion that this kind of rivalry brings is always so big that it is almost compulsory to take an interest.

Tonight will be slightly different for me because I will come up against one of my compatriots and someone who I know well. Ralf Rangnick does not need to read these pages to know how much I like and respect him, but I should say it anyway for the benefit of others.

Firstly, because it is true but also because it is important that all of us can demonstrate that underneath the rivalry, the passion and the desire to win, it is always possible to have a healthy respect for our opponents. This, for me, is what sport is about.

Ralf took over as manager when United were in a difficult moment but I know from my experience of him that his work will be beneficial in the long term. Ralf has never just worked for today or for short-term results, he has always looked to get solid foundations in place so that the club he works for has a positive future.

This, I would say, is very smart as well as being good news for Manchester United. So I welcome Ralf to Anfield as a friend and a rival. I look forward to being in his company and I know that he will want to be on the winning side just as much as I do. Neither of us would have it any other way.

I know that there will be some who will look at the result last time our two clubs met and will view tonight's fixture as a foregone conclusion. I cannot help those people and I am glad that we will have no-one like this in our dressing room.

I also know, having spoken to some of the people involved, that even when Liverpool were dominant in the 1980s, United were always their toughest opponent. Again, this is because of the rivalry and I expect tonight to be no different.

April 2022

Past results do not matter. Form does not matter. Placings in the league table do not matter. The only thing that does matter will be the way we approach the game on the pitch.

I love this. I love the fact that giving everything and being brave in a football sense is what gives you the best chance of being successful in fixtures like this one. We alone are responsible for our performance and we will embrace this responsibility in the same way that we always do.

Unfortunately, print deadlines mean I am writing these notes ahead of our FA Cup semi-final against Manchester City so I am not able to refer to the result of this game whether it was the one we hoped for or the one we hoped to avoid. What I can do, though, is thank our fans for their efforts in getting to Wembley Stadium to support the team.

I know this was not an easy trip for many, many reasons so the appreciation that I always have for our supporters is even greater than it normally is. For us as a club, these are special times because we have made good progress in all four competitions, but we also know how demanding all of this can be for our supporters. I can assure you this will never be taken for granted.

It is a challenge for all of us in different ways so the best thing we can do is try to enjoy it together and see where it takes us.

Liverpool 4, Manchester United 0

Goals: Diaz (5), Salah (22, 85), Mane (68)

Line-up: Alisson, Alexander-Arnold, Matip, Van Dijk, Robertson, Henderson, Fabinho (Milner 86), Thiago (Keita 80), Salah, Mane, Diaz (Jota 70). Subs not used: Konate, Gomez, Jones, Tsimikas, Origi, Kelleher

Jürgen's post-match reaction: 'We were top level and that's very important. We started the game well and finished the game extremely well. In between we had a spell where we had to adjust to the different high-press system, line-up and organisation of the opponent. But it's really difficult, we were 2-0 up. I saw so many football games when one team was clearly better. We were clearly better in the first half. Then keeping the concentration level is, obviously, very important but then we have a 15-minute break and we go out and the opponent is going for it, but I thought with the first ball we passed through the lines [and we] could turn in the centre again, from that moment on we were again completely in charge. So, yes, top class performance, absolutely. My moment of the game, even when it was very important and a great result, was the seventh minute when our people showed pure class. The whole stadium together showed pure class [in a minute of applause following the death of Cristiano Ronaldo's baby son], in a moment where we obviously, everybody knew since yesterday, since I heard first time about it, so many things they are much more important in life +than football. Obviously, we really feel for Cristiano and his family. That was my moment of the game, but other football moments were obviously absolutely outstanding.

Yes, Mo scored two, set up the first. Luis set up Sadio's and got the ball from Mo, and all these kinds of things. Diogo came on, set Mo's second up, all these kinds of things, [it] couldn't have been better to be honest. Yes, Thiago played a good game. That's his quality. With quality obviously comes responsibility, so if you are good you better play good as well. That's what he did tonight really, again. From a football point of view, really nothing to moan about. It was the perfect night for us, we don't take these kinds of things for granted.'

Post-match notes

When the clock reached seven minutes, both sets of fans led a minute of applause following the death of Cristiano Ronaldo's baby son. In footballing terms, the Reds became the first team in the Premier League era to score at least eight goals against Manchester United in one season following the 5-0 win at Old Trafford in October. This victory took the Reds to the top of the table and mathematically ensured they will play Champions League football again next season. Mo Salah's double meant he became the first Liverpool player to score five league goals against Manchester United in a single season. Sadio Mane's strike meant he has now scored as many Premier League goals as Ryan Giggs – but in 374 fewer games. The four goals the Reds scored is more league goals than Manchester United have managed at Anfield during Jürgen Klopp's time at Liverpool.

v Everton
Sunday, April 24th, 4.30pm

‘IT’S SO IMPORTANT TO ENJOY A MOMENT THERE AND THEN, RATHER THAN WHAT IT COULD LEAD TO’

Premier League

April 2022

GOOD afternoon and welcome back to Anfield for our Premier League fixture against Everton. I welcome Frank Lampard, his players, staff, officials and the supporters of our visitors.

It's great to see Frank back managing again, in our league. I think it's often underestimated what a great job he did at Chelsea. They are still benefiting from the decisions he made and specifically the young talent he developed while in charge there.

I think it's often forgotten that initially they were under a transfer embargo when he arrived, which would have made the job of leading a top club, with that level of expectation, even more challenging. It's difficult to judge properly from the outside, but I thought he and his staff did an outstanding job during that period, as Frank did at Derby County before that.

We've seen in fixtures recently, including this week against Leicester City, that Everton under Frank are a team that will fight and battle until the very end. Their motivation today will be at the highest level possible, so we have to be ready for that.

We come into this game after an important result for us in midweek. The performance from the team and the crowd was of the highest level. But we will need exactly the same again today, if not more.

The best word I can think of to describe the situation at the moment is relentless. Manchester City at

Wembley in a cup semi-final, then Manchester United a few days later…now Everton. I'm not complaining for one second and it's a situation we have fought hard for. But it is relentless and therefore we need to be also.

The intensity of these games is not an issue. It's something we crave actually. The more intense the game, the more it usually matters. The intensity reflects how important all these contests are. As with the feeling of relentlessness, it's about us matching the situation with our performance.

I want us to continue to be relentless and intense on the pitch as a team. Be the guys who give everything in each moment – not just for spells but constantly. Individually and collectively give all you have in that moment and then do it again and again.

Likewise from our supporters. The atmosphere being created at the moment mirrors the performance of the team. The noise being created is relentless and intense. The boys are feeding from it.

Just as important as throwing everything into each individual fixture is making sure we then take the maximum experience from it, when our efforts bring rewards.

Every media interview at the moment focuses on what might be and that's fine because that's our world. Anticipation and expectation is absolutely okay, even though for us as a team it is irrelevant. And as I've said repeatedly, it's the supporters' job to dream and ours to deliver.

What I've really loved about how we've collectively enjoyed moments in recent weeks is that it reflects our mindset of being in the 'now' at all times.

Take the semi-final at Wembley last weekend, as an example. Our supporters extracted the maximum amount of joy from the entire experience. This was evident the whole day, not just because of how the game or result went. And these moments and memories are ours forever now, irrespective of the outcome in the final.

It's so important to enjoy a moment for what it is there and then, rather than what it could ultimately lead to. Because you can't go back and have that moment again retrospectively. I love that we do this together.

Of course for the players and management staff we have to draw a line quicker and re-focus, but that's how it should be. The boys do this so outstandingly well. They dwell on nothing a second longer than is necessary, good and bad.

This is evident in matches. We have a good moment, we don't bask in it, we go again and chase another one. We have a setback, we don't wallow in it, we immediately look to strike back. And this is the relentless attitude on the pitch we must continue to show.

Today's game will be incredibly hard. It will likely be

95 minutes long as a minimum. For each second the game is active we all need to be on our toes. We must not pause or stop. Players and supporters, together, bringing intensity to Anfield and being relentless in our approach.

I know the ground today will be full of passion and it's something that makes fixtures like this so incredibly special.

However, to finish this column I do feel the need to address something which has surfaced in recent games which should be a cause for concern for any right-minded, compassionate person, regardless of which team they are associated with.

Throughout my career as a player and a manager, I have always tried to be as positive as I possibly can be about football supporters. Not for PR or for selfish reasons; it is because, more than anything else, I am a football supporter myself and because I know the unbelievable difference that fans do make to a sport that I absolutely love.

I never expect perfection but I always believe that in general supporters will be a force for good because that is almost always what they are. Which is why I am unbelievably disappointed that of late we have heard more and more songs being sung about the Hillsborough disaster. Really? The deaths of 97 people in a tragedy is now something that can be mocked?

How did this happen? We have staff at the club who lost loved ones at Hillsborough. There are supporters in the crowd at all of our games who lost friends or family members themselves or who survived the tragedy. They have already suffered more than enough.

No-one should think it is okay to make them suffer more because it absolutely is not.

I know there will be some who will say, "But what about this and what about that?" So I will say this very clearly: if you are going to a football match to sing about people losing their lives you really should not bother coming. Football does not want this and football does not need this.

As ever, but especially at this time of year, the Hillsborough families and survivors are in the thoughts of everyone at Liverpool FC and I want you to know that you have our total support on this and every other issue.

Liverpool 2, Everton 0

Goals: Robertson (62), Origi (85)

Line-up: Alisson, Alexander-Arnold, Matip, Van Dijk, Robertson, Keita (Origi 60), Fabinho, Thiago, Salah, Mane (Diaz 60), Jota (Henderson 82). Subs not used: Konate, Milner, Gomez, Jones, Tsimikas, Kelleher

Jürgen's post-match reaction: 'Div is a legend on and off the pitch, I have to say. That's how it is. He is a fantastic footballer, for me, and I know that sounds ridiculous because I don't line him up often. He is a world-class striker, he is our best finisher, definitely; he always was and everybody would say the same. When you see him doing these kinds of things in training and then he is not in the squad because of the quality of the other players, that is really hard. I can imagine today again, other players were not in the squad, they are in a really good shape, they are really hard decisions to make because the boys all want to contribute and all are responsible for the situation we are in. Div, everybody loves Div and rightly so. He was again very decisive and I'm very, very happy for him.'

Post-match notes

Divock Origi was the man for the big occasion again, netting his sixth league goal against Everton. That was his 11th goal as a substitute in the Premier League, more than any other Liverpool player.

April 2022

v Villarreal
Wednesday, April 27th, 8pm

'YOU WON'T WIN GAMES LIKE THIS BECAUSE OF WHAT YOU'VE DONE IN THE PAST AS A CLUB'

UEFA Champions League semi-final, first leg

Jürgen Klopp

GOOD evening and welcome back to Anfield for our UEFA Champions League semi-final against Villarreal. I welcome Unai Emery, his players, staff, officials and the supporters of our visitors.

What a remarkable job Unai is doing again. Of course this is not a surprise. He is regarded as one of the very best coaches in the world for a reason. He is an incredible leader of a football club. Domestically for sure but crucially, given the competition in which we face each other tonight, European football also. What he has achieved so far in his career can only be admired and there is clearly so much more to come.

Our respect for Villarreal as an opponent could not be higher. They are elite. They are reigning Europa League champions and they have been formidable in the Champions League during this campaign.

I hate that part of the external narrative around this match will probably have been a debate about whether or not Villarreal have been and will be underestimated. Honestly, anyone who suggests this to me ahead of our fixtures against them knows absolutely nothing about this group of players, us as management staff, or our club in general.

We come up against a team of proven winners. They have world-class players, a world-class coach and a home stadium where they harness and deploy the passionate support they have. They are the complete package.

As a team and a club we have been blessed to enjoy some fantastic experiences together in European competition since I arrived here and we managed this because we always respected our opponents' strengths while not ignoring our own qualities. That will be the case tonight. It's always the balance to strike.

It's not a case of 'fearing' Villarreal or their talent. This is never our mindset. But we know to have any chance of progressing beyond the semi-finals we must show our best face for the entirety of this contest. Every second of it. We cannot switch off at any moment, or we could be done. We have to use all our own tools. We have to work harder than them. We have to be braver and more committed. It's that simple.

So we will focus on ourselves and what we can do.

The match at the weekend was a good example of how important it is to keep the focus on yourself and trust your own abilities.

I know there was a lot of conjecture around certain incidents in the game, but the reality is we thoroughly deserved to win over the course of the 90 minutes. We dominated in my view. We have definitely played better in matches than we did on Sunday, both recently and over the course of the season, but at this stage of the season it really is about showing the 'street-smart' to ensure the end outcome is what you are working for.

What was key, is that in the face of high pressure and

an opponent giving all they had, we didn't lose belief in ourselves and we remained patient. We trusted ourselves. This was the case on the pitch and in the stands. I loved it, actually. It was a group of players and supporters showing a total understanding of the situation in front of them.

We are going to need to be exactly the same tonight. We know whatever happens this tie will be alive going to Spain for the second leg. So absolutely nothing will be decided tonight, in either direction. That's important to acknowledge. What we can do this evening is try and win a football match. That would be cool I think.

As the team and as supporters we can ensure that when the final whistle goes around 10pm this evening we have done all we can to win on the night. We don't need to worry about the ultimate outcome of the tie just yet. All our focus needs to be on this game and this game only. Ninety minutes plus stoppage-time tonight. A Champions League semi-final, under the lights at one of football's great cathedrals.

Turning back to our opponents, without wanting to dwell on them, there is a member of their squad we will be delighted to see again, because he is a very important part of our club's recent history. Alberto Moreno is a person and player we miss so much at Liverpool and it is a real shame that he will be unable to feature tonight as he is currently recovering from an injury.

Alberto is a wonderful player, a wonderful person and the contribution he made to our club was immense. He brought energy to our group each and every day. He made coming into work for everyone just that little bit more enjoyable.

I miss having him in our group to be honest, but equally I couldn't be happier to see the success he has had at Villarreal. He deserves it. A special guy with big talent. I wish him nothing but great moments for the future. There is still a lot to come for him.

And speaking of people who deserve special appreciation, I have to talk about Divock Origi.

His performance on Sunday in the derby was top-drawer. But it's exactly what we expected. He trains each day to the highest level. He is in the best shape I have ever seen him if I'm being honest.

It is by some distance the toughest part of my job having to disappoint people who don't deserve it when it comes to team and squad selection. It's a luxury problem to have and I wouldn't change it, but at the moment I have about 23 players who are all performing at a level which means they should start matches. Unfortunately this isn't possible.

But the responsibility the players have, to themselves and the club, is to always be ready to contribute when time on the pitch in matches presents itself. Divock grasped his and then some! I love how appreciated he is here, by everyone. I love how much affection there is for him.

If these do prove to be his final weeks and months with Liverpool Football Club he is continuing to work and perform in a manner which reflects the status we all hold him in. And that status is club legend to be honest.

I hope there are more 'Divock moments' between now and the end of the season. But regardless, how he conducts himself and how he contributes to our club each and every day at the training ground, no matter how limited his opportunities have been until now, speaks volumes for him as a man and a professional. I could not appreciate him more.

Finally, I referenced the performance on and off the pitch on Sunday earlier in this column and it's the impact of Anfield I want to return to.

We all know the phrase 'famous European night' is synonymous with our club. But it is like this because we never take it for granted. We know it's not an entitlement. Anfield doesn't come alive on these occasions because of bricks and mortar or floodlights or the name on the stand. It's about the people. It's always about the people.

If we want tonight to be special for all the right reasons we have to work for it. From the moment we enter the stadium until the moment we leave. You won't win games like this because of what you've done in the past as a team or a club. You don't have a special atmosphere because it was like that when our parents and grandparents came. No matter how recent. It's what you do on the night.

We are currently writing our own history and that's really cool. We can make tonight another memorable chapter in it if we are all humble enough to work incredibly hard to make it so. And that's players, management and supporters.

Let's give everything and enjoy this experience together.

Liverpool 2, Villarreal 0

Goals: Estupinan (53og), Mane (55)

Line-up: Alisson, Alexander-Arnold (Gomez 81), Konate, Van Dijk, Robertson, Henderson (Keita 72), Fabinho, Thiago, Salah, Mane (Jota 73), Diaz (Origi 81). Subs not used: Milner, Adrian, Oxlade-Chamberlain, Minamino, Matip, R Williams, Kelleher, Elliott

Jürgen's post-match reaction: 'Nothing happened yet, that's how it is. For me, it's the best example, you play a game and it's 2-0 at half-time [then] you have to be completely on alert. You have to be 100 per cent in the right mood, you have to play the second half like you played the first half. There is nothing to defend [and] if you do that you [lose] immediately all the advantages you might have had before. We know we go there and it will be a tricky atmosphere for us and different from tonight. Their players, you saw it tonight, they fight with all they have and what I like [is] that everybody could see that we fought with all we have. It's always the same. If they beat us with a result that brings them to the final, then they deserve it and if not then we deserve it. That's how the competition is. We played a really good game and now in five days we will play again and we have to make sure that we are ready.'

Post-match notes

Liverpool made it nine wins in this season's Champions League, the most games they have ever won in a single European campaign. Villarreal's one effort on goal was the joint-lowest in a Champions League semi-final match since records began.

In the afterglow of the Villarreal game, Liverpool fans were given another reason to celebrate – but this time it wasn't because of the result of a game. Their beloved manager would be trying to bring them success for four more years...

'DO I HAVE THE ENERGY TO GIVE THIS AMAZING PLACE WHAT IT NEEDS? I'M IN LOVE WITH HERE AND I FEEL FINE'

What Jürgen said after agreeing to extend his Liverpool contract until 2026...

"There are so many words I could use to describe how I am feeling about this news... delighted, humbled, blessed, privileged and excited would be a start. There is just so much to love about this place. I knew that before I came here, I got to know it even better after I arrived and now I know it more than ever before. Like any healthy relationship, it always has to be a two-way street; you have to be right for each other. The feeling we were absolutely right for each other is what brought me here in the first place and it's why I've extended previously. This one is different because of the length of time we have been together. I had to ask myself the question: Is it right for Liverpool that I stay longer? Along with my two assistant managers, Pep Lijnders and Pete Krawietz, we came to the conclusion it was a 'Yes!' There is a freshness about us as a club still and this energises me. For as long as I have been here, our owners have been unbelievably committed and energetic about this club and it is clear that right now this applies to our future as much as I've ever known. In Billy Hogan and Julian Ward we have leaders throughout the club who are completely focused on renewal and refreshing so we can continue to compete at the very highest level. We have managed to harness the best of what we have created already at the same time as injecting fresh impetus into our environment. The new AXA

Training Centre is a superb home for us and the fact that Anfield will grow even bigger soon with the Anfield Road development, I can't wait for that. We are a club that is constantly moving in the right direction. We have a clear idea of what we want; we have a clear idea of how we try to achieve it. That's always a great position to start from. When the owners brought the possibility to renew to me, I asked myself the question I've mused over publicly. Do I have the energy and vibe to give of myself again what this amazing place requires from the person in the manager's office? I didn't need too long to answer in truth. The answer was very simple… I'm in love with here and I feel fine!"

Fenway Sports Group's Mike Gordon said…

"It's always hard to find the right words to adequately reflect Jürgen's importance and contribution to our club, but today's announcement really does speak for itself. But speaking on behalf of my partners John [Henry] and Tom [Werner], as well as myself, Jürgen is the perfect figurehead for the modern Liverpool FC. This is especially true of what he stands for, on and off the pitch. It also applies to the leader he is and the man he is. Because of our extraordinary playing squad, outstanding coaches, world-class football operations team and brilliant club staff, we are blessed with the most valuable resource an organisation could wish for: amazing people. Everything Jürgen has said publicly about his future previously was reflected by his words privately to us. It was about him having the inclination and desire to keep going. In this respect, it is clear he is more energised than ever. What our latest agreement gives us, across the organisation, is an opportunity to benefit from continuity, particularly in terms of renewals, whilst retaining and, where possible, enhancing our keen focus on refreshing and reinvigorating at all times. As Jürgen has himself alluded to, we have incredible talent across the club, led by Billy Hogan and his executive team for the wider business. Plus, more specifically for football, Julian Ward as sporting director, football ops and the wider AXA set-up, including our sensational Academy. It's a talent pool that is incredibly deep and totally committed. Jürgen wanting to make our future to be as bright as our present is a big statement. We cannot rest or consolidate. We have to think at all times about improvement and we are now able to do this in the knowledge that we have retained a manager who not only shares our vision and ambition, he remains determined to deliver on it. For these reasons and many more, it is beyond thrilling to know Jürgen Klopp will lead us into this new era."

Saturday, April 30th, 12.30pm
Premier League
Newcastle 0, Liverpool 1

Goal: Keita (19)

Line-up: Alisson, Gomez, Matip, Van Dijk, Robertson, Keita, Henderson (Fabinho 69), Milner (Thiago 78), Diaz, Jota, Mane (Salah 69).
Subs not used: Konate, Jones, Tsimikas, Kelleher, Alexander-Arnold, Elliott

Jürgen's post-match reaction: 'I thought it was a top-class game in extremely difficult circumstances. That's why I'm really happy. You want to win football games and in the best case you deserve to win, and we did today 100 per cent against a team in great form in a great atmosphere. It was incredibly difficult for the boys today, to be honest, it's clear. We played two and a half days ago. Coming here, a team in form, six home wins on the bounce, everybody in a good mood, pretty much everything was prepared for another home win. The only group who wanted to avoid that was my players. It was an outstanding football game.'

Post-match notes

This win at St James' Park moved the Reds to top spot in the Premier League – until Manchester City's win later on. It was Liverpool's 42nd victory in the 2021-22 season.

MAY

2022

And so a season that would ultimately include 63 games drew to an exciting climax. A Champions League final was reached but ended in disappointment, while 92 points wasn't enough to win the league title. But with the FA Cup added to the trophy haul, Klopp could be hugely satisfied with his team's achievements

3rd: Villarreal (CL) A
7th: Tottenham (PL) H
10th: Aston Villa (PL) A
14th: Chelsea (FA) N
17th: Southampton (PL) A
22nd: Wolverhampton W (PL) H
28th: Real Madrid (CL) N

May 2022

Tuesday, May 3rd, 8pm
UEFA Champions League semi-final, second leg
Villarreal 2 Liverpool 3
(Liverpool win 5-2 on aggregate)

Goals: Fabinho (62), Diaz (67), Mane (74)

Line-up: Alisson, Alexander-Arnold, Konate, Van Dijk, Robertson (Tsimikas 79), Keita (Henderson 79), Fabinho (Milner 84), Thiago (Jones 80), Salah, Jota (Diaz 46), Mane. Subs not used: Gomez, Oxlade-Chamberlain, Minamino, Origi, Matip, Kelleher, Elliott

Jürgen's post-match reaction: 'Outstanding, massive, it feels like it's the first, to be honest, because it is always so special. It is, for me, the best club competition in the world. I love it, love the sound, everything, love the nights. Respect to Villarreal, this really wonderful stadium, what the people are doing here is incredible, what Unai [Emery] is doing is incredible, how the players put us under pressure, everything is great. So it feels so special because it was so difficult for us, but in the end we deserved it as well and that's really cool. It was massive, massive from the boys. Before the game I told the boys that I would like to read the headlines that 'The mentality monsters were in town' just because I wanted us from the first moment not to look like somebody that defends the result but goes for the three points or for the win. I couldn't see that but the second half was like this... for me it was like this because you could see how impressed we were in the first half and then coming back like we came back in the second half was really special. With the 500 games, like it feels, that the boys played it is completely normal that the first half can happen but reacting like we reacted made it really special again and it is that that we are really happy about. There's only one chance to win a final and that is to qualify for a final. That's what we did so far, we played each game available. We went through all competitions until the last game, three of these competitions are not finished yet. In the first half today a lot of people might have been happy that we got a knock, but it's really difficult to reach three finals – that's probably the reason why nobody did it so far. But we made that happen and when the specific finals show up in our schedule we will make sure that we are ready. But we play incredibly strong teams in these finals. We will give it a go, definitely, but that it's difficult I could have told you without knowing that nobody did it so far.'

Post-match notes

The 5-2 aggregate win ensured the Reds reached their 10th European Cup final. They became the first English club to reach the final of the European Cup, FA Cup and League Cup in the same season. Jürgen Klopp became the fourth manager to reach four European Cup finals after Marcello Lippi, Alex Ferguson and Carlo Ancelotti. Three goals in Villarreal meant the Reds reached 139 for the season – the most the club have ever recorded in a single campaign.

v Tottenham
Saturday, May 7th, 7.45pm

'NOTHING BUT LOVE AND RESPECT TO THE PLAYERS FOR HOW THEY HAVE NAVIGATED THIS PERIOD'

Premier League

GOOD evening and welcome back to Anfield for the Premier League fixture against Tottenham Hotspur. I welcome Antonio Conte, his players, staff, officials and the supporters of our visitors.

What a job Antonio has done since returning to this country. His record in general is not to contest. He's a winner. A fantastic leader of a football team. My respect for what he has done in his career and continues to do could not be higher.

You don't have to do too much analysis on Spurs to see Antonio and his staff have already put their stamp on the club.

Like us, they have the highest possible motivation to secure points in this game. It is clear the Champions League qualification will go down to the wire and they will give all they have to try and finish in the top four. We must be ready to face a team who will fight for everything, in every moment.

Our games versus Tottenham are always super competitive anyway. Since I have been here we have had a proper rivalry but always based on mutual respect, I think. I can't remember a game against them not being enthralling to be honest. So a really cool fixture for everyone. Can't wait.

Of course we come into tonight after a big week. I don't want to dwell on the semi-final win in Villarreal because our focus must switch immediately. However,

I cannot ignore it. Nothing but love and respect to all the players for how they have navigated this period and Tuesday night in particular. What we are involved in at the moment is insane if you pause and think about it for a second. It's a blessing for us that we have no time to pause. We just have to keep going. Never stop.

The match wasn't straightforward but nor did we expect it to be. It was as tough and intense as you could imagine a Champions League semi-final to be. After the game there was a lot said about us reaching our third European final in five seasons, but that's not something I really thought about. For me it feels like our first and I love that. And it has to be a similar attitude for everything we are involved in. It will help keep us energetic and fresh. Treat everything as a new opportunity.

The turnaround to this evening is short but again this is not to present an excuse, it is just a fact. We are used to it now – it is our life. It's a challenge for many factors, not least the quality of opponent we will come up against, but I have total belief in this group. Players and staff. They are so mentally tough and resilient. I could not be prouder.

It is the first home game since my staff and I decided to extend our contracts with Liverpool, so I want to address that in this column.

There is no secret why. We are in love with this place.

And that connection is very much centred on people.

I have just written about the players and they are a huge factor in this. They are just the most incredible set of boys. From the oldest to the youngest, they inspire me each and every day with their talent and application.

As a manager or coach you are only ever as good as your playing squad. I have been blessed in my career to have worked with some amazing teams and be part of remarkable dressing rooms; Mainz and Dortmund but also during my earlier time here. This current one I would struggle to better, for sure.

It's not just that they are fantastic with a ball at their feet, or in their hands. That helps for results, yes. But it's also the men they are. Coming into work with them is a privilege. They are the reason we are enjoying these fantastic experiences together.

I hope I never have taken them for granted and never will. It is not possible for them to all be as happy and positive about me all the time, because I have to disappoint on occasions when it comes to team selection. That is a manager's life. But I think I can confidently say we trust each other. And that's a critical thing in any relationship: to trust in each other.

It's very similar with the amazing club staff we have. These are the guys who prop us up. They put us on their back and carry us when we need them to. Their contribution is off the charts. I cannot start listing names, it makes no sense, but they carry value to LFC that should not be underestimated.

To have colleagues who you can also count as friends is something very special in life. For me it is even more than friendship. We have a sense of community. It's very special. And knowing that we will be together for longer brings a joy that beats any trophy we've won.

And of course I cannot understate our supporters. I know every manager talks up their team's fans and – as with the playing squad – I've been blessed to enjoy an excellent relationship at my two previous clubs also and I hate that sometimes you are asked to compare. It is not to compare. Each is unique.

The bond we have here, though, is something I could not have envisaged. It's authentic, it's real. It feels like we really appreciate each other. And that's not specific to me – I am only a small part of it. It's the team and the staff as a whole. We believe in each other and take energy from each other.

As a manager you can never make promises of success, it's not possible. It applies to the remainder of this season also. We don't know what will happen with the competitions we remain active in. But you can do everything within your own capabilities to make sure we at least throw all we have at it, in each moment.

It's what we've done until now and I think it makes sense to keep doing it. It's why all these special relationships feel so fresh and can continue to feel fresh into the next few years. Be it players, staff or supporters, I want us to attack each day like it is our first together and could be our last together.

This evening is a perfect example of where we will need it. If we come together and give our all we can ask nothing more of ourselves. And we should do it as a collective.

I hope we can make it a special night.

Liverpool 1, Tottenham 1

Goal: Diaz (74)

Line-up: Alisson, Alexander-Arnold, Konate, Van Dijk, Robertson (Tsimikas 64), Henderson (Jota 65), Fabinho (Keita 88), Thiago, Salah, Mane, Diaz. Subs not used: Milner, Gomez, Jones, Origi, Matip, Kelleher

Jürgen's post-match reaction: 'It is an important point because we have one point more than before the game, so that's how it is. But we all know the situation. We are now top of the table. If you ask me, my favourite situation, it just stays like this with the same points tally, and City and us, we lose all the rest of the games in the Premier League and it stays like this. That would be great, but we all know it will not happen. So in this moment, we are disappointed. The boys are more disappointed than I am – it might be because of my age, because I saw pretty much everything already in my life. But we will go again. There were so many good things tonight in a situation like that. The counter-press we played today, you can record it and sell this stuff, it's unbelievable. Honestly, it's unbelievable. I am so proud of that but, in the end, in the little moments, a little bit better decision-making... it's easy for me to say because I don't run and I didn't run four days ago, but we all know the boys are able to do that and then we could have won. But, of course, we know we could've lost as well because they are obviously insane in their counter-attacking. That's what they want to do. I saw a lot of the things we want to do but not the result we wished for.'

Post-match notes

This draw stretched the Reds' unbeaten Premier League run to 16 games (13 wins, three draws) and put them top of the Premier League on goal difference. Luis Diaz scored in back-to-back games for Liverpool for the first time.

Tuesday, May 10th, 8pm
Premier League
Aston Villa 1, Liverpool 2

Goals: Matip (6), Mane (65)

Line-up: Alisson, Alexander-Arnold, Matip, Van Dijk, Tsimikas, Keita, Fabinho (Henderson 30), Jones (Thiago 62), Diaz (Salah 72), Mane, Jota.
Subs not used: Konate, Milner, Firmino, Gomez, Origi, Kelleher

Jürgen's post-match reaction: 'We needed time to find our way into the game and the opponent was there from the beginning, like really aggressive, a lot of challenges. On top of that, we were 1-0 down. In the last 10 or 15 minutes of the first half we started controlling the game and that was then the way we had to do it. Scored the second – incredible goal, top-class. If my players would not be as good as they are I would talk about completely different stuff with you. Their quality, mentality and character is the reason why we are where we are. I'm not surprised they are able to do something like this but I don't take it for granted – I'm really proud tonight of the boys, it was massive. I invited the boys to follow my [thinking]. In my mind, we were six points behind City before the last matchday and then we won and they lost and we were only three points. I came here today with that mindset, it means we are still chasing like mad. Honestly, maybe because I'm a bit dumb, but it works brilliantly for me! And the boys are invited to follow that path. We don't waste energy to think, 'Hopefully they lose' or whatever. No, we just know we have to win, that didn't change at all. Now we have to recover, really recover and then to play the FA Cup final because there's obviously no mercy anywhere. We caused this situation ourselves by qualifying for all finals, which is absolutely massive. And now we play an incredibly big game and from Thursday on we'll prepare that with the boys.'

Post-match notes

The Reds came from behind to win, meaning they had gained 14 points from losing positions in the Premier League this season – the most in the division.

FA CUP
L.F.C.
AXA

‘WE ARE SO INCREDIBLY CLOSE WITH EACH OTHER AND OUR FANS – IT’S A PURE JOY TO BE PART OF THIS CLUB’

Saturday, May 14th, 4.45pm
FA Cup final
Chelsea 0, Liverpool 0
(Liverpool win 6-5 on penalties)

Penalty scorers: Milner, Thiago, Firmino, Alexander-Arnold, Jota, Tsimikas

Line-up: Alisson, Alexander-Arnold, Konate, Van Dijk (Matip 91), Robertson (Tsimikas 111), Keita (Milner 74), Henderson, Thiago, Salah (Jota 33), Mane, Diaz (Firmino 98). Subs not used: Gomez, Jones, Origi, Kelleher

Post-match notes

Liverpool beat Chelsea on penalties in a final for the second time this season, winning the FA Cup for the first time since 2006. Jürgen Klopp became only the second manager to win the European Cup, league title, FA Cup, and League Cup with the same English club.

Jürgen's post-match reaction:

On how much it means...

"My team knows exactly what I think about them, that's the most important [thing]. This is again a trophy for the whole club – of course for the team, but for the whole club. We saw before the game already what it means to the people because our hotel is pretty central, we saw them all partying already since this morning. When we came into the stadium and looked at all the faces, like when we came to the bus, we could see what it means to the people. On the pitch with the performance you saw what it means to the players. It's unbelievable, it's massive, it's game number 60 or whatever in a very, very intense season, and putting out a performance like this is absolutely incredible. But most important – really most important – I have to say all respect to Chelsea. What a team, what a performance. In the end we all know a penalty shoot-out is a lottery. But we did it again. We work together with a company – four guys, their name is neuro11. I got in contact with them two years ago, I think, got aware of it. One of them is a neuroscientist and he said, 'We can train penalty-shooting'. 'Really?' I said, 'Sounds interesting, come over'. German guy, we met, we worked together and this trophy is for them obviously as well, like the Carabao Cup was. Sadio's penalty is for sure at least 50 per cent my responsibility because you have to let the boys do what they think they do, but with him I said, 'He knows you exactly, the goalie, so do the other way around'. How very often in my life, I realised it's better to shut up! But we still made it and honestly it means the world to us. It was difficult. The first 25 minutes were the best 25 minutes we played ever against Chelsea, we played an incredible game, but we didn't score. Then it's clear, Chelsea with the quality they have, they find a way back in the game. There were ups and downs in the game. They had their chances, we had massive chances, none of us used them. So a penalty shoot-out is a logical thing. Doing it like this feels good but gives you more a sense of how hard it must be for the opponent, because it would have been extremely hard for us in that moment after 120 minutes, losing like this. So, honestly, my respect to Chelsea and what they did."

On the players' special stories...

"That we won now both domestic cups, that really is special. That Trent Alexander-Arnold is the youngest player ever in this incredible history of the Premier League who won all six major trophies, at 23, the youngest. So many special stories. And after the game I said to Thiago, 'If I would have known what a player you are, I would have signed you four years earlier'. He said, 'You taught me running!' I take that, it's fine. He could obviously already play football pretty well but he learned running in Liverpool, that's fine. So many special stories, Jordan Henderson obviously and these kinds of things. It's really cool. James Milner, at a quite advanced age having such an impact on a football team. Let me say, we had to change Mo early, which was not cool. It was my decision, it was pretty precautionary. Mo said, 'I feel something, [but] I can carry on'. I said, 'No'. A football game is not a perfect physiotherapist, it means it rarely gets better during a game. Then Virg stands with me and says, 'I feel something but it's fine I think'. We make a decision together, so he stays on but was clear when we didn't make it in 90 minutes he has to go off. Then you can bring Diogo Jota and Joel Matip on in this moment – that's the best situation I've ever been in as a coach, to be honest. That's absolutely outstanding, that's why we had the chance to go for it. It was difficult, we know that. It was lucky, we know that. But we deserved it as well and that's really cool."

On having no time to celebrate...

"The best physiotherapist is winning football games, to be honest. Robbo had a cramp, so that's obviously normal and completely fine. I was surprised that more players didn't have cramp, to be honest, after what we had to do tonight. So before you are in a situation, you never know exactly how big it feels. It feels massive. I cannot believe it. It feels massive. The only problem I have is that we cannot really celebrate it because we play on Tuesday. I think: how can you do that? It's such a fantastic competition, such a fantastic occasion and then you limit the celebration – okay, obviously not for the people, they can do what they want – but for the team by putting in a game on Tuesday. It is like it is and from here we go."

On the contribution of man-of-the-match Luis Diaz...

"What a boy, what a story, what a player [Luis Diaz is] – but he should have scored! I think we agree. He agrees probably. So the speed he has is insane. Not to forget, he played on the side of Chalobah and Reece James and getting in a situation like this is absolutely unlikely. The big chance he had in the first half, I think it was a pass from Trent – if you want, we can talk about his performance as well, by the way – and he should have scored in that moment with his quality. That's how it is. But what a player. He's outstanding. He's a fantastic boy. It's so funny, so we hug each other after the game and just shout 'Vamos!' and whatever, the few words I know in a similar language. But he gets our football 100 per cent. We thought we saw that at Porto but that it's really like this, I feel really lucky as well, to be honest. He fits like a glove to our football and that's really, really special."

On his team's place in history...

"I don't have to make this decision [about where this team ranks among the greatest ever] and I don't have to judge this and have to think about that. Other people have to do that. I couldn't care less, to be honest. I enjoy the moment with these boys. We are so incredibly close with each other and with our fans – it's a pure joy to be part of this club in the moment. There's a lot to come and a lot to play for, we all know that. But for tonight I decided to take that and just enjoy this moment and don't think about the next challenge we are facing. Because it's really special, it's really special. Imagine, like 20 years ahead and then you look back... Jordan Henderson is probably then a pundit or maybe not even a pundit anymore because he thought that makes no sense anymore, so in 20 years then you think: he's the captain of the only Liverpool team so far – hopefully not the only because maybe we can do it again, which will be completely ridiculous – but he was the first captain who won four trophies, as an example. The Trent story. All these other stories. Where Virgil van Dijk was six years ago in his career when he thought: where will it go? When we go five years back, Ibou Konate probably played in the under-16s of whatever team in France. And now we are here for this moment. We don't finish, it's just now for the moment a little reflection. But we don't have to decide where this team ranks. I know a few players of these teams but I cannot say how they played. But I'm pretty sure in the time when they played, they were the best teams. But meanwhile, we know so much more about training, we know so much more about sports science, all these kind of things. That's why these boys are obviously much fitter than the former generations were – it's nothing to do with football talent or whatever. If the players from the past, like Rushie or Kenny, if they would've been trained like the boys are trained today, imagine that? That would be crazy. So, it's all good for the moment. We don't stop here, we just take the time to enjoy it for a few minutes. We came from a season last year where nobody thought, I'm 100 per cent sure in this room nobody thought, apart from me maybe, that we can go again like we did this year. That we could do it is all because of the character of these players – it's the only reason. Because I can say whatever I want, I can motivate as much as I want, [but] if these boys don't listen, if these boys are a little bit distracted by whatever or get weak or soft or whatever, then in this moment you don't have a chance… But today is FA Cup and we won the game and we have the medal, a wonderful T-shirt. That's enough for the moment."

The players' post-match reaction:

Jordan Henderson:

"It has completed the set of everything [European Cup, Premier League, UEFA Super Cup, FIFA Club World Cup, FA Cup and League Cup as captain] but it's not really about me to be honest. It means the world to captain this team and to lead this team at Wembley was extra-special for me and I thought the lads were incredible. So I'm really delighted. I think the win sums this group up and it gives us a boost. We've played a lot of games in a short space of time and you can see a few of the lads struggling with little niggles and stuff. Mo came off today and Fab in the last game and then big Virg also came off before the extra-time. The FA Cup is a big trophy and we haven't won it for a long period of time at this club so that will give us a big boost for the rest of the season. Ali has been incredible since he came to the club. He made another world-class save in the penalty shoot-out and even in the game itself he made one or two good saves. He's made a big difference since he came in, of course, and for me he's the best keeper in the world. The fans were incredible again. It was the same in the semi-final and in the Carabao Cup final here. It makes a big difference for us when you're out on that pitch and it was great to be able to celebrate another trophy with them."

Fabinho:

"I was really nervous. I was talking to someone and I said when I played in the Carabao Cup final I was confident, but outside of the pitch it is really different. We played a really good game and we had chances to win the game in normal time, but we did not take them. They had really good chances as well and it wasn't easy to watch this game. It was a really good game of football – both teams played a really good game – and I am happy because we won the FA Cup. Luis [Diaz] showed his quality again. I think he was the man of the match and in the first half the best chances that we had came from his foot. He could have scored one or two times and he tried to pass the ball one time to Thiago. He wants the ball so the players are giving him the ball because we know he can create good chances and do something special because he is a special player. He didn't score today, but he showed he has really high confidence and hopefully he will continue playing like this. Now I am really looking forward to playing in Paris in the Champions League final. I am really confident I will be fit to play and help my team-mates. We are working hard on treatment and the medical staff are doing everything possible to make me fit. I am really looking forward to it and to helping the team."

Sadio Mane:

"It is so special. Our target at the start of the season was to win trophies and so far we have two and we will see if it is possible to win more. For my penalty, we [Edouard Mendy and I] know each other. He is my friend and teammate for Senegal. His left side is not his best side so I tried to put it there, but he saved it. I'm happy for myself though because at the end of the day we won the trophy."

Alisson Becker:

"We did such a good performance. It's a shame that we didn't score during the normal time but it was a proper fight and in extra-time anything could happen. We kept the clean sheet and brought it to the penalties and then afterwards the boys, they were unbelievable with scoring the goals and then I just needed to save the last one. I'm so happy. I think all the goalkeeper coaches, they helped me with the decisions. In the end I am there, I need to make the decision myself. Chelsea did really well but we deserved the win. I did that save because we deserved to win this."

Kostas Tsimikas:
"We have to celebrate hard, but tomorrow is the next day and we still have a lot to do. It's very, very special for me. The manager asked me which number [penalty] I want. I said number seven. He said why so far? I said [that] number seven gave me the opportunity to win the game, I chose the right side and I scored – very, very happy for that. I'm not a Greek Scouser – I'm the Scouse Greek! We have to celebrate now but still we have to be 100 per cent focused if we want to achieve our goals."

Trent Alexander-Arnold:
"Honestly, it's always tight when we play Chelsea. We just can't get the better of each other – it always comes down to pens and draws. That's four draws now [this season]. It's hard to beat them but we were resilient and we've got the job done when it matters. We've kept

calm under pressure and slotted our pens. We made changes. Things didn't go our way during the game but we adapted, we dealt with it and we played the game how we needed it to be played. We didn't let them do what they wanted to do. As the game went on, they kind of took more control of the game, but that first half was again very good from us and we just couldn't put the ball in the back of the net. We had the chances to do so but couldn't quite do it at the end of the day, but that doesn't matter to us. Penalty shoot-outs are tense but you get up there, you are focused, you know which way you are going to go and you commit to it. That's all you can really do, and try to hit the ball well. It's easy to over-complicate things but you are 12 yards out, just strike the ball well and you've got a decent chance of scoring, so that's what I did today."

Tuesday, May 17th, 7.45pm
Premier League
Southampton 1, Liverpool 2

Goals: Minamino (27), Matip (67)

Line-up: Alisson, Gomez (Henderson 46), Matip, Konate, Tsimikas, Elliott (Origi 65), Milner, Jones, Minamino, Firmino (Keita 83), Jota. Subs not used: Thiago, Oxlade-Chamberlain, Diaz, Robertson, R Williams, Kelleher

Jürgen's post-match reaction: 'I think [it was] an incredible performance, making nine changes. If it wouldn't have worked out it would have been one thousand per cent my responsibility. Now, it worked out and it's one thousand per cent the boys' responsibility because I can ask for a lot, [but] the boys have to do it. I saw incredible performances tonight. We played in all the spaces they couldn't get us. So, that calmed the atmosphere down, obviously, and it became more a normal game and not the game Southampton wanted. Fantastic, absolutely fantastic.'

Post-match notes

Liverpool made nine changes but still moved to within a point of Manchester City with one game left to play. They remained the only team unbeaten in the Premier League in 2022. Joel Matip has been on the winning side in all eight league matches in which he's scored for the Reds.

Jürgen Klopp

v Wolverhampton W
Sunday, May 22nd, 4pm

'WE HAVE ESSENTIALLY REACHED THE FINAL OF EVERYTHING. I AM SO PROUD OF OUR CLUB'

Premier League

May 2022

GOOD afternoon and welcome to Anfield for our final Premier League game of the season, against Wolverhampton Wanderers. I welcome Bruno Lage, his players, staff, officials and the supporters of our visitors.

What a season Wolves have had. They are a brilliant football team with big talent and a proper work-ethic. I am very pleased for Bruno. I don't know him personally but he's done a fantastic job this campaign and is clearly a cool, thoughtful guy.

He's been coaching a very long time, at various levels and different roles so it is easy to have a huge respect for him. He has a clear idea of how he wants to play and his players respond to that. It sounds simple but it isn't.

Our match at their place earlier in the season is one of the toughest we faced in all competitions. Not that we need a warning sign but we have a personal memory to draw from so it makes sense to use it.

Wolves will be exactly the same today, I'm sure. Resilient. Organised. Determined. Full of purpose. Full of ambition. Full of quality. I should also mention their captain, Conor Coady, who has all of these qualities and more. I have no doubt that the staff at our Academy who remember him will be unbelievably proud of the player that Conor has become. He is the symbol of a great club and our admiration for him and his achievements is absolute.

From our perspective I can't be any clearer in my

message: our focus is here. Our focus has to be here. If we can't win this game then nothing else matters. Winning here today is a hard-enough task. We will need to give everything. We will need to be patient and smart. We'll need to work harder than them.

Our minds, our bodies, our everything have to be entirely at Anfield. I know I don't need to give this team-talk to players or supporters because they'll know their job. Make our home a cauldron of positive energy. Make it fizz. Make it buzz. It's for us to do it on the pitch and our people from the stands.

I want us all in 'work mode'. We have a job to do. And then, when the work is done, we can all show appreciation for each other. Then we can celebrate with each other, regardless of the outcome. Honestly, if we all give everything for the match, at its conclusion we can have nothing but pride irrespective of outcomes elsewhere. This is my wish for today.

We have essentially reached 'the final' of everything we have competed for. Two domestic cups, the European Cup – and to take the Premier League campaign to the last match round is the equivalent of reaching a final.

Saying how proud I am of our team and our club is an understatement.

I said on Tuesday night, shortly after the win at Southampton, that I felt quite emotional. And I did. I was choked-up, to be honest.

This was mainly because it was a perfect case-study of how together we are as a club. All of us. We all contribute. We all play our part. We are such a powerful collective. The players who came in, who have been denied more minutes this season not because of lack of ability or effort but simply the restrictions of the team-sheet, showed the world what I see every day. They are warriors. They make us what we are.

Likewise the supporters who came to St Mary's. The away end. Wow. After all the travelling, spending, time off work…all the sacrifices to follow and support us…they were on their toes and our twelfth man from beginning to end. They are not to compare.

And this team is not to compare. I was asked after the FA Cup final win where I thought this Liverpool team ranked among the greatest in history. I can't remember what my answer was but given where my head was it probably wasn't impressive. And I get this question a lot.

So let me answer now: it's unique and does not need to be pitted against any other.

Because this team, this set of players, are all about the present. We respect our past and we are excited for our future. But these special, special, special boys are about the here-and-now. They live for the moment.

It's why they've achieved such remarkable things this season already. It's why when the whistle goes for kick-off everything that has gone before won't matter and everything that could come after will be ignored. They will play the moment right in front of them. They will compete like crazy. It's what they do. They're my heroes, to be honest.

I said earlier, when the work is done we should celebrate each other and show appreciation to each other regardless of what the ultimate outcome is. It's so important. We are a community.

And it's important I use this column, on behalf of all the staff and the players, to pay tribute to the even tighter group we have around us as individuals, and that's our families.

Without the support of those who love and care for us at home we would be nothing. I know I would be lost for sure. Without Ulla and my two boys, I would be nowhere. They make it all make sense. And it's the same for all of us so privileged to work here. Our families make sacrifices so we can shine. For us, days like today are about showing appreciation for them also.

None of us can make promises this afternoon beyond the commitment we make every day that we represent Liverpool Football Club and that is to do our very best. We give all we have and see what happens. But one thing is for sure: we won't ever give up. We won't give up in games. We won't give up on competitions. We won't give up today. We won't give up next season either.

Or the seasons after that. This club never gives up. We keep going. Sometimes we suffer together, sometimes we share joy together.

For us it's always about the journey. It's a shared journey. It cannot be taken away from us and presented to someone else and engraved with their name on it. This is ours and we should cherish it.

From my heart, which is full of love and anticipation, I thank everyone who's joined us on the journey this season. You've been great travelling companions. And we haven't finished yet.

Liverpool 3, Wolverhampton W 1

Goals: Mane (24), Salah (84), Robertson (89)

Line-up: Alisson, Alexander-Arnold, Matip, Konate, Robertson, Keita (Firmino 70), Henderson, Thiago (Milner 46), Jota (Salah 58), Mane, Diaz.
Subs not used: Van Dijk, Jones, Minamino, Tsimikas, Kelleher, Elliott

Jürgen's post-match reaction: 'The boys played an incredible season, the whole journey of 2021-22 so far is absolutely exceptional. I think the game today showed again so much about these boys. We concede an early goal, which gave us a knock, I have to say. Didn't play football really, not like we usually play. Have to take off Thiago early, which is not helpful. Then you still find a way – it's absolutely outstanding. 92 points obviously is crazy with all the games we played. So, yes, I am proud but I'm disappointed of course as well. There are maybe worse scenarios; if you would have been a point up and don't make it, that might feel even worse. But apart from that, it's not cool. But it's not completely unexpected obviously, it was clear before the game that a lot of things had to happen. I don't want to forget it, I said it in all interviews and will say it here as well of course: congratulations to Man City, Pep Guardiola, all staff, all players, whole club, for being champions. We were close but in the end not close enough. That's how it is. The season was so close, so tight, moments, decisions, these kinds of things, when you are one point only apart. What I learned about life is if you stay on track, if you keep going, you get the reward. Not today, the maximum reward. But we will get it. It's about us to keep going and that's what we will do. This season is absolutely incredible and will not end today, it ends next week obviously. And there we will try absolutely everything. This season is incredible, absolutely incredible. And of course, losing the league today increased the desire to put it right next week.'

Post-match notes

Liverpool lost out on the league title by one point but finished on 92 points. Mo Salah became the fourth player to finish the Premier League season top for both goals and assists. He also collected a third Golden Boot. Only Thierry Henry (4) has more. The Reds finished the season unbeaten at home in the league, the fifth time they've done so in the PL era. Alisson collected the Golden Glove award, finishing level with Manchester City's Ederson with 20 clean sheets apiece in the league.

Saturday, May 28th, 8.36pm
UEFA Champions League final
Liverpool 0, Real Madrid 1

Line-up: Alisson, Alexander-Arnold, Konate, Van Dijk, Robertson, Henderson (Keita 77), Fabinho, Thiago (Firmino 77), Salah, Mane, Diaz (Jota 65). Subs not used: Milner, Gomez, Oxlade-Chamberlain, Jones, Minamino, Tsimikas, Matip, Kelleher, Elliott

Jürgen's post-match reaction: 'After the game when I saw the stats it was 50-50 possession. We had a lot more shots, a lot more shots on target, but the most decisive stat is absolutely on Madrid's side. Just to make sure that nobody thinks I wouldn't congratulate Real Madrid, I do that now but I [also] congratulated everybody present and involved outside personally. They scored a goal, we didn't, that's the easiest explanation in the world of football and it's hard, harsh to get anyway, [but we] respect that of course. When the goalkeeper is Man of the Match then something is going wrong for the other team, so we had, I think, three really big chances where Courtois made incredible saves. I would have loved to have had a few more of this calibre. We had the best phase probably after they scored the 1-0, then we played immediately exactly in the spaces we had to play. In the first half there were good moments, when we found Sadio, next left to right from Casemiro, their centre-halves stayed deep, Sad could turn, arrived in the box. That was good. We wanted to play a bit more in their formation in the second half than around their formation. The problem is when you play against Real Madrid and they defend that deep, the counter-attacking threat they are is immense. I saw us doing really a lot of good things but it was not enough and we take that. They scored and we didn't. We could have played better football but Madrid could have played better football but they didn't and they won anyway. Madrid played already a lot of games better, we can now say they played exactly like they have to, fine, that's how you play a final. If we didn't want the ball then we would have both played in our halves and that is not possible. Again, the stats is 50-50 possession so it was not that they never had the ball, absolutely, but apart from the goal they didn't have a shot on target – that is a good sign for my team. We had nine shots on target, that is really a good number, but the problem is they scored with one shot and we didn't score with nine. That's the difference.'

Post-match notes

Vinicius Junior's second-half goal decided a match that Liverpool dominated for large spells with Real Madrid goalkeeper Thibaut Courtois earning the man of the match award. Jordan Henderson became the first Englishman to captain a team in three different Champions League finals. Liverpool FC formally requested an investigation into security failures outside the stadium that created huge issues for thousands of Liverpool fans as they tried to gain entry into the stadium. Those problems resulted in the match kicking off 36 minutes later than originally planned.

May 2022

An incredible 63-game season may not have had the dream ending it deserved, but Jürgen Klopp could still be proud of his team. A parade through the streets of Liverpool the day after the Champions League final proved the fans were equally proud of the players' efforts. The boss was given the chance to reflect on a remarkable journey...

Klopp on the season overall...

"These boys played an outstanding season. The two competitions we couldn't win, we didn't win for the smallest possible margin – one point, 1-0. What does that say? [Manchester] City during the season were one point better and tonight Madrid were one goal better. That says nothing about us. The difference between 2018 and now is that I see us coming again. In 2018 I wished it but I couldn't know. But these boys are really competitive, they have an incredible attitude, it's a fantastic group and we will go again definitely. It's an unbelievable season. What the boys did is unbelievable, what the coaches did is unbelievable. The concentration we kept up, the level we kept, unbelievable. All good. Now I have a holiday!"

Klopp on his emotions during the parade…

"Without a shadow of a doubt, no club in the world – this world – that they lost the Champions League final the night before and the people arrive here in the shape they are, the mood they are. Absolutely outstanding. This is the best club in the world – I don't care what other people think!"

Klopp on the players being nervous about what to expect from the parade…

"I wasn't sure what we can expect. We spoke about it before, 'What do we do?' You have to plan this kind of thing. You can't just decide to have a parade. But I hoped that we find something like this, it's absolutely incredible."

Klopp on wanting his players to enjoy their achievements…

"That's the biggest sign you can give to the world. Yes, we won two competitions, great, but we didn't win the last two – and these people don't forget, they know exactly what a shift the boys put in. Absolutely incredible. It's such a boost for everything that will come. Unbelievable."

Klopp on his pride in the squad and the supporters…

"I'm proud of the players but I'm proud of these people, to be honest. Unbelievable. Yesterday in the stadium some things happened that nobody understood, our families were in trouble, all these kinds of things. Now we come here and see this, when you see the eyes of the people, it's incredible. That's the best sign you can get: you don't have to win, you just need to put all that you have in, really throw everything on the pitch and the people of Liverpool love you. We celebrate life, we celebrate the season, we celebrate our competitions, we celebrate the championship [of 2020]."

Klopp's final message…

"I love you all! And I'm not drunk, not a little bit, just emotional!"

SEASON STATISTICS

The numbers that sum up the long and successful season Jürgen Klopp and his team steered the Reds to

Season statistics

Appearances (all competitions)

Name	PL	FA	LC	Europe	Total
Jordan Henderson	35	5	5	12	57
Diogo Jota	35	5	4	11	55
Alisson Becker	36	4	1	13	54
Mohamed Salah	35	2	1	13	51
Virgil van Dijk	34	5	3	9	51
Sadio Mane	34	3	1	13	51
Fabinho	29	3	3	13	48
Andy Robertson	29	4	4	10	47
Trent Alexander-Arnold	32	3	3	9	47
Joel Matip	31	1	4	7	43
Naby Keita	23	4	3	10	40
James Milner	24	3	4	8	39
Thiago Alcantara	25	4	0	10	39
Roberto Firmino	20	5	3	7	35
Alex Oxlade-Chamberlain	17	2	4	6	29
Ibrahima Konate	11	6	4	8	29
Curtis Jones	15	4	4	4	27
Kostas Tsimikas	13	5	3	5	26
Luis Diaz	13	5	1	7	26
Takumi Minamino	11	4	5	4	24
Joe Gomez	8	2	4	7	21
Divock Origi	7	1	3	7	18
Harvey Elliott	6	3	1	1	11
Tyler Morton	2	2	3	2	9
Neco Williams	1	0	4	3	8
Caoimhin Kelleher	2	2	4	0	8
Conor Bradley	0	1	3	1	5
Kaide Gordon	1	1	2	0	4
Nathaniel Phillips	0	0	1	2	3
Elijah Dixon-Bonner	0	1	1	0	2
Owen Beck	0	0	2	0	2
Max Woltman	0	1	0	1	2

Melkamu Frauendorf	*0*	*1*	*0*	*0*	*1*
Harvey Blair	*0*	*0*	*1*	*0*	*1*
James Norris	*0*	*1*	*0*	*0*	*1*
Billy Koumetio	*0*	*0*	*1*	*0*	*1*
Adrian San Miguel	*0*	*0*	*1*	*0*	*1*

Goals (all competitions)

Name	***PL***	***FA***	***LC***	***Europe***	***Total***
Mohamed Salah	*23*	*0*	*0*	*8*	*31*
Sadio Mane	*16*	*2*	*0*	*5*	*23*
Diogo Jota	*15*	*2*	*3*	*1*	*21*
Roberto Firmino	*5*	*1*	*0*	*5*	*11*
Takumi Minamino	*3*	*3*	*4*	*0*	*10*
Fabinho	*5*	*2*	*0*	*1*	*8*
Divock Origi	*3*	*0*	*2*	*1*	*6*
Luis Diaz	*4*	*0*	*0*	*2*	*6*
Naby Keita	*3*	*0*	*0*	*1*	*4*
Joel Matip	*3*	*0*	*0*	*0*	*3*
Jordan Henderson	*2*	*0*	*0*	*1*	*3*
Andy Robertson	*3*	*0*	*0*	*0*	*3*
Alex Oxlade-Chamberlain	*2*	*0*	*1*	*0*	*3*
Virgil van Dijk	*3*	*0*	*0*	*0*	*3*
Ibrahima Konate	*0*	*1*	*0*	*2*	*3*
Own goals	*0*	*0*	*0*	*2*	*2*
Trent Alexander-Arnold	*2*	*0*	*0*	*0*	*2*
Thiago Alcantara	*1*	*0*	*0*	*1*	*2*
Harvey Elliott	*0*	*1*	*0*	*0*	*1*
Curtis Jones	*1*	*0*	*0*	*0*	*1*
Kaide Gordon	*0*	*1*	*0*	*0*	*1*

Players transferred in for/during 2021-22

Ibrahima Konate	*RB Leipzig*	*July 2021*
Luis Diaz	*Porto*	*January 2022*

Trophies won

Carabao Cup
FA Cup

Premier League Player of the Month awards

October	*Mohamed Salah*
November	*Trent Alexander-Arnold*
February	*Joel Matip*

Jürgen Klopp awards

League Managers' Association Manager of the Year
Premier League Manager of the Year

Stats from the 2021-22 Premier League season:

– Mo Salah finished joint-top scorer in the league with 23 goals.

– Salah also finished top of the assists chart with 13, ahead of Trent Alexander-Arnold (12).

– Alisson was the goalkeeper with the joint-highest number of clean sheets, claiming 20 (equal with Ederson) in the league.

– With 92 points, the Reds would have won the Premier League title in 23 of the previous 29 seasons.